AF284965

Günter von Hummel

'tea-drunken'

Essays from the tripartite unified Human

The cover picture shows the Machapuchare, an almost eight-thousander in the Himalayas. I did not climb this mountain, of course, but I hiked towards it and this tour was one of the most impressive ones, which also inspired most to the meditative-psychological reflections of this book. On the second page of each chapter I show a picture of the corresponding title.

© 2022, Günter von Hummel
Printed and published by:Books on Demand,
Norderstedt, Germany
ISBN 9783755726463

Table of Contents

Introduction

My didacting analyst O. Count Wittgenstein, from whom I received the important, practical part of my psychoanalytic training, wrote a book: "sagen, hören, sehen" (saying, hearing, seeing) with the subtitle "Vom dreiteiligeinigen Menschen" (From the tripartite unified Human). In it he used myths and fairy tales as well as philosophical and psychoanalytical forms of observation to formulate what he called a 'trialogical' goal. The picture below from his book shows this in an overview for the time being.

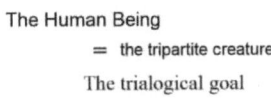

The Human Being

= the tripartite creature

The trialogical goal

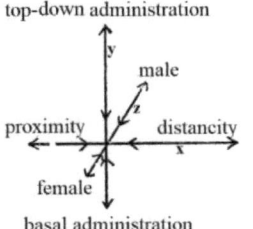

top-down administration

proximity

distancity

female

basal administration

connection   of the x-axis = communication level
of the y-axis = level of power
of the z-axis = sexual differentiation
with respecting reversible tendencies

x – distance and relationship
y – reciprocal top-down and basal administration
z – Bi-, Mono- und Hetero-Sexualität

realized: Woman - Man - Child - Unity
introjected: Soul - Spirit - Body - Unity
projected: Holy Trinity

'Trialogical' should mean that the 'tripartite' human being can find unity through a special kind of communication or through the 'logical practice' of psychoanalysis in the form of a tripartite logo and not only of a dialogue. It is not enough that only the therapist and the patient sit together, there has to be a third being or a third in the sense of the trialogue: S. Freud for example or the consensus of the psychoanalytical teaching. Only in this way, by means of a psychoanalytical 'working through' of the same tripartity of the X-, Y- and Z-axes, can a person arrive at self-unity in a comprehensive form. For man is not, of his own accord, a self-sufficiently resting personality. In this book I am also concerned with this 'tripartite unity', whereby I would like to assign the mountain hikes to the 'seeing' of Count Wittgenstein's book title, the meditation to the 'hearing' and the knowledge, the science, to the 'saying'.

In this way I want to convey Count Wittgenstein's 'tripartite unity', but also the tripartism in other ways than only scientifically, namely by incorporating physical and meditative exercises. The last step, the 'trialogical goal', should be transferred to Count Wittgenstein accordingly and transferred to concrete lives, in approximately at the end of the second life-thirds be reached. By then one should have reached the point where one can reconcile the many opposing aspects shown in this illustration. Sometimes Count Wittgenstein meant already the phase after puberty to reach the 'trialogue', i.e. the stage of life where one has really overcome this phase. But even this phase, called postpubertal, can be completed quite late in life. Unfortunately, the postpubertal phase can also be found in many adults. In order to accelerate the process of maturity, it is therefore necessary to take some physical effort (e.g. hiking in the mountains) and meditation into psychoanalysis.

As mentioned above, 'trialogical' should also mean that one has to go beyond the mostly deceptive 'dialogue', which is understood here as a conversation between two people, to a 'three-way conversation', in which a reference to the unconscious, to the completely Other in ourselves, yes to the foreign in us as a third party is included. All the world today speaks of dialogue and thinks that it is possible to grasp everything interpersonal in full depth with it. However, Count Wittgenstein believed that one can proceed from the catalogical (the pure listing of handles) to the analogical (the entirely similar) and only then come to the real and true dialogical. It is therefore a three-step, three-conversational, psychoanalytic process to the true dialogue, which Count Wittgenstein just called 'trialogue'.

In a conversation Count Wittgenstein once indicated to me that he wanted to introduce the concept of 'trisexuality' in order to be able to expand Freud's basic assumption of a bisexuality that is invested in each human being. I found this curious, and I believe he never again announced or published anything in this direction, as much as the concept of 'trinity' - as just described - is important for psychoanalysis and ultimate maturity. Nevertheless, today I can get a better idea of what moved Count Wittgenstein at that time. There are too many sexualities, which Freud mostly characterized as 'infantile' and which man should transform through cultural development. Now remnants of this infantility remain in all forms of sexuality, even in heterosexuality, which is superficially classified as normal, a man who constantly needs another woman and has ten others in mind is problematic, neurotic, not to say perverted. And so I consider the 'trialogue', in which it also refers to the sexual, to be a good term, because man is not only born with immature sexuality and remains imprisoned in it, but also with an immature 'logos', a very rudimentary ability to say and speak, which he does not bring to full development.

In addition to the descriptions of various walking tours, I would also like to weave in remarks about a meditation that uses psychoanalysis as a scientific basis, but manages it without too much complex theory. I have reported in many non-fiction books about my own meditative method. However, because of their scientific pretensions, these reports sound very sober and no less complex than today's psychoanalytic literature, in which the many schools of thought can only with difficulty agree on a common set of terms. Nowadays psychoanalysis is too institutionalized, and so there is too much 'discomfort' in its culture, as Freud already complained in his time.

To return to 'seeing' and the mountain hikes: From the top of the mountains, one usually sees well into the distance, but at the same time one should also look at oneself in one's own inner proximity, because only in this way do outer and inner perception, which I also call the image-real, come together. And with the 'hearing' I connect the word-real correlating with it, which mainly refers to psychoanalysis, but also to what Count Wittgenstein indicated with basal and top-down administration. For as I understand meditation, this word-real comes more from above, from the top-down administration, supplemented by psychoanalysis, where it seems to come from below, where man is virtually administered by his unconscious desire, because he can only badly defend himself against these strivings from there.

After all, 'saying' will not only refer to science, but also to the relationship between man and woman, which is otherwise known only from hundreds of novels or from one's own life, which may not have been entirely successful. Nowhere is 'saying' so important as between the two sexes, where one thinks one already knows and knows everything about the other, thinks one has already discussed this with one's life partner and many other people, and yet nothing changes and improves. That's why the other part of psychoanalysis is in demand here, namely the one with which she claims to be a science. Here everything must be questioned exactly and only with love and good intentions alone it is not done. So it is precisely where intimate life is concerned that science is called for, albeit in a particularly human dimension.

Furthermore, it is not easy to integrate the other aspects of the realized, introjected and projected X-Y-Z-axes into the assignments of the X-Y-Z-axes, which are listed in the above illustration. The affiliations of both the axes and their designations overlap with so many parameters. And so I will try to think about sexual differentiation in my mountain hikes, as well as about top down management and administration in case of too close proximity. The ultimate goal is the 'trialogy' anyway, to which I will try to head over several chapters. I will include further remarks in the following texts.

1. Tramin - South Tyrol

You can climb the Roen directly from Tramin, four hours circa to the top. At the beginning, everything seems to go quite comfortably. A bit hilly, a dew-covered meadow, a forest, a small stream and a few swampy spots. At first the grass seems almost a little malachite green with a few marsh marigolds and restharrow herbs in between. But after that, the trail winds up the dark green forest. No one walks on this path, a few birds chirp, you are alone. At one point a small snake slithers by the side of the path and quickly disappears into the bushes. Two black beetles race on a tree bark. The times are probably long gone when one had to be afraid of larger animals in the forest. There are also no dangerous people to be expected. Yes, no people appear at all anymore. Almost no one knows this direct route, and apparently no tourists at all.

You can feel as if you were the owner of a large area of trees, branches and bushes and of a spicy-scented coniferous soil. It smells of the essential oil of spruces and larks, and I imagine that the earth here tastes a bit tart, clayey and just like ancient, healthy forest grounds. All this together results in something contemplative, in a mood of connection, in a 'perceptual identity'. Sigmund Freud contrasted this with the 'thinking identity' that we use today. In the 'perceptual identity' one feels identical with the wind, which plays around one, blows around one, breathes around one, and the soft coniferous soil, the diatomaceous earth of the stones and the humming of the small animals close as seldom else. But we modern people no longer smell and taste, nor do we grasp anything with the inner touch, as the philosopher D. Heller-Roazen called it.[1] Rather, we immediately have something linguistic and conceptual at hand when it comes to what we take to be 'true'. In short: instead of the more pictorial, 'imaginary order', the image-real, we prefer the word-like, 'symbolic order', the word-real, and above all we do not reconcile the two. Precisely for this a third element is needed, which I want to create by my procedure.

It goes now steeper uphill. From time to time rocks can be seen, then it goes again through the high treed forest, a narrow path further and further up. Nevertheless, again the impression, you are master of the world, everything leans towards you, cooler mountain air spreads and gives the lungs a refresher. Still, it's not much fun. The path is

---

[1] Heller-Roazen, D., The Inner Touch, Der innere Sinn, Archeology of a Feeling, fischer wissenschaft (2012)

exhausting and only after three and a half hours you reach a small plateau from which a via ferrata continues up. It is one of the usual metal ladders, not too difficult. Maybe even a little highlight, and then you're at the top. There's a bit of snow even in June, but again - at least at the time I was there, around 1965 - no people.

Just for this view into the vastness, into the endless valley, and for this being lifted off from all the hustle and bustle below, one has gone up. Deep down you can see lively green of various shades and the glittering flowing water of the river Adige. Many houses, farmsteads, wine terraces, orchards. Micro-vehicles, micro-people, micro-things and micro-animals moving along the streets below. Is this really the show, the painting, the vision you expected of life? For fitness, it was quite good to go to the top, but otherwise? Somewhere I hope from such a hike, without people work, without big meetings with other people, without small talk and also without other events, to meet the very big. Why should that not exist, that after a hike, after a lot of nature, effort, a great view and a few good thoughts and 'lifts up' something charismatic happens?[2]

But I am not a gusher, I hate these tree-whisperers, the excessive nature-enthusiasts, these neo-animists who

---

[2] I will come back to the concept of charisma. I do not want to use it theologically or in a too everyday human way, but I want to keep it on a middle level, on which also psycho-analysis is located.

believe that matter is alive.[3] Their books are quite amusing and also interesting to read, but why do they have to come along so warm-heartedly, as if this autochthonous enjoying were not already in us and there even much more vividly experiencable? A few people come to my memory, even directly to my inner gaze, and I think the thoughts that were shared with them. They live partly no more, partly the thoughts were not so important. For what then were the people actually there, for what were the words exchanged?

Hard to bear how insignificant we all are, but there must be something else, nothing 'spiritual', rather something 'beyond our sentences', as the philosopher M. Foucault complained. Something different of our I-being, the image-word-real in the Other of the unconscious.[4] Probably the word charisma is too strong for that. It would be enough if one could only return a bit to the perceptual identity and understand the view from above as an overflight, an overview of the essence of the world. However, the whole thing would then have to be held together - now I am going very far ahead - by a kind of an 'overword'. Because the view weakens in the memory, but the word remains. It remains at least somewhat longer and also more precisely in the memory.

---

[3] Bennett, J., Vibrant Matter, John Hope Franklin Center Book (2010)

[4] Psychoanalyst J. Lacan calls the image-word-real the unconscious important Other, who is the main psychic instance through internalizations of significant others outside.

But since I don't have the 'overword' available yet, I want to forget first of all all this giant background of culture, religion, politics, sciences and what God knows what else is talked and done. I just wanted to talk about being up there, to have a little far-sightedness and to be content with the feeling of being alive. Breathing by itself is grandiose. But it's not enough and so I wrote it all down. Probably no one will read it, it will not be the great true. I repeat, the great truth must exist somewhere. Inside us, around us. It is good to remember it, for a moment, maybe. After that, you descend from the Roen another way. Towards the Mendel Pass, it is easier to walk. You reach a bench, a small sign of grace, sit down, close your eyes and wait.

Soon after, the silence begins to make itself felt. Never is the silence completely still. But the distant sounds of life down in the valley are even conducive to meditation. Fine rubbing, rustling and humming noises put even the smallest children into relaxation. You can even place an electric toothbrush near them to help them fall asleep more easily. And so the sounds of the human world coming from far away are also calming, and after a while a fine sound can be heard inside, as if one were concentrating on it. At the same time it is he who concentrates on me, and he becomes clearer and clearer.

Above, above and to the right in the head or in the depths of the brain or the unconscious, he emerges. Lacan refers to him as something 'real'.[5] I have been meditating in this way for a long time, it is nothing special, the sound, tone or something similarly audible is carried by everyone. It is something vertical, as if one is plumbed in the sound, graded, up, down, down, up. If one has practiced a lot with it, and listens to it longer, it gets the character of something that wants to be heard, that wants to make itself noticeable and say something.

This is nothing pathological. At some point it becomes clear that it is one's own unconscious thoughts that become quite easily audible, that one can almost hear and then also suddenly almost thinks one can understand. They are not the usual thoughts that one thinks. Maybe they are no thoughts at all or only preforms of them, but at the moment of their increasing being grasped they are unconscious thoughts, they are even consciously understood. This does not mean that one fully comprehends them. They do not attain the form of a story, a prolonged expression, or even a revival. They are not charismatic, not the great true or the very great at all. But they do exist in real terms. The unconscious is the treasure house of signifiers Lacan claims, central place of units of interpretation, of directives, of riddle words, signs and slogans, of the unconscious other to be writ large, which has arisen in us internalized by the sounds of the envi-

---

[5] The 'real' according to the French psychoanalyst J. Lacan is not the inner or outer reality, but something that stands opposite the 'imaginary' and 'symbolic order' as a third.

ronment, parents, teachers, analysts, in short: all this significant Others.

Often it deals just with insignificant memories, fantasies, which are immediately wiped away. Sometimes, however, peculiar sayings come to light, of which one has the feeling that they could really tell one something. Something essential. You then have to have good rationality to really focus only on the few clear and good syllables, half-sentences or saying-like thoughts. Clear ratio is needed as well as the irrational of the unconscious. In such moments there is no more question about the great true, because there is at least something corresponding to it. It is perhaps not great, this true, but there is something about it. As said it distributes instructions, revelations and even sometimes slogans.

From Roen you can also walk along the ridge to the Überetscher hut, then take a chair lift for a bit and finally reach the Mendel pass, from where a path leads again to the funicular to Kaltern. Again and again new, fantastic views into the valley show up. Somewhere off the path I stop again on a tree stump. It takes some time again, until in the silence a cloudy, concentrated something is established in the head, from which the said sound stands out and in this medium, in this inwardly expanding darkness, becomes an announcement. One cannot say from where exactly it comes, but now, in the silence where I sit there, the consciousness immediately grabs this approach of syllables or already almost whole words and makes a half-sentence out of it, or even more.

"Tea-drunken" I suddenly hear inside me, "tea-drunken"? Strangely, quietly and as if coming out of the depths of the bodily unconscious. It was quite clear, I did not mishear: "tea-drunken", what is that!? The rational immediately intervenes and sorts out in a matter of seconds whether what I have heard is nonsense or has hidden meaning. Can one get drunk on tea? Maybe, but I think the meaning consists of a more figurative sense. It is quite clear what it means, because when it comes from oneself, one usually knows it immediately. For me it had the meaning of a drunkenness through meditation in general, in which one does not become drunk from what usually makes one drunk. Such a drunkenness from nothing is often claimed.

Medieval mystics and Asian wisdom teachers mention such phenomena with words like sartori, samadhi or ecstasy. They are intoxicated by God, they say. I call such a thing a simple catharsis, a self-sublimation, a relaxing abreaction, the perception of a slight "trickling through" in the body image, a liberating switching in the neuro-psychic system, which then opens a channel for hearing thoughts. It is often the case in the normal state that one does not know whether a thought comes entirely from one's own ego or was triggered from somewhere else.

Despite everything: "tea-drunken" was a good and beautiful word, I thought to myself as I continued to walk down into the valley. My rationality told me it was okay. Because it is simply about something other, the Other as such, and less about all those giant background and foreground noises that I just mentioned we are usually at the mercy of: the clatter of the world, of politics, of people, of everyday problems. The silence somehow becomes audible in the moments when one relaxes and sinks a bit into inner contemplation, into leisure. And then it sometimes lets through a signifier that comes as if from afar or from the depths, an effective image-word-real that has meaning.

That long lasting silence starts to drone, as one says, is of course only true under the condition that it is tense, e.g. when people sit together because of a problem and nobody says anything. But in the situation when one rests exhausted from the hike, the silence rather begins to whisper, murmur or sound like thoughts.

On from above or right above as I claim is not to mean neurological orientation. It probably has only incidentally to do with the nerve junction that the left-brain speech center has an effect to the right. It also has something to do with the word association centers or simply the meaning context in which one is associated with others. Lacan says it are the echoes, unconsciously accumulating in the body, of all that is audible and heard that comes forward. It is the same with the usual whispering, when one cannot be sure what one has heard, as in the game 'whispering mail': the associations then begin to speak themselves.

Of course, one can also be drunk on tea, if one is a very special connoisseur of certain teas, of "Golden Assam" for example, or of "Kusmi Darjeeling" or any other second-flash product of recognized teas. But just then the drunkenness is only an additional emergence from the ceremony of tea preparation and consumption. It is a matter of psychological exaltation, of hyperthymia. I am a tea drinker, have also looked forward to tea after my hike, but translate the whole thing primarily as a metaphor for my attempts at meditation, for self-drunkenness, which is a meditation of the Other. I don't like artificial exaggeration, and I also always write the word 'spiritual' in quotation or interrogative marks.

That is to say, I do not get into ecstasy, not into a frenzy. One experiences something like that, which is perhaps a little mysterious but still easy to interpret in any good meditation. But it must be said, heard, thought as if set apart from any conscious thought, and understood rather as if from afar, from the depths or seemingly alien. That something speaks from the unconscious is a thing in itself. Something or someone wants to tell me something here that has just been circulating repressed or even split off in the unconscious and finally had the opportunity to burst forth. Wittgenstein would have said that it comes out of the conflictual tripartite and wants to express itself in a logo, a motto, a nimbus, a proper name unifying everything.

So what? "Tea-drunken" is not that strongly revealing. Or is it? I should write about it, it should be about writing down again, I couldn't discover any other sense - except that of catharsis, and that it is typical of meditation. Maybe I'm obsessive about writing, too. I've written thirty books about my psychoanalytic-meditative process, and I'm sure I've published over a hundred articles on the Internet about it. I am letter drunk, writing drunk, sharing drunk, that will be it. And it's enough, I shouldn't write more, it won't do. I'm not just drunk on tea leaves - that too to some extent - but on writable sheets of paper, printed pages, books and internet pages. I need to reduce the drunkenness, even if it's nice and my books can't say it all.

In any case, "tea-drunken" does not come from the Wittgensteinian `top-down-aministration' above, nor from the `basal administration' below, or from far or near. It has come from the middle, where it is really meditation, charisma, something between the 'saying' and the 'hearing'. And so I had to get up and also continue down the path into the valley to Tramin. Once down there, I immediately sat down at the typewriter and wrote these lines. At that time there were no laptops with voice recognition and other bells and whistles. You had to type flawlessly. You couldn't insert, change, and delete vocabulary in the text like you can on a PC today. Still, the fun was the same.

So after that, a tea. It was a tea from Sri Lanka, where we, family and friends, among others, once visited the tea pickers in the highlands. They seemed so humble and strong and at peace with themselves. But when we wanted to give them some money, they completely lost their dignity and fought greedily over the bills. It was not much that we gave, and we were struck by the obvious blatant poverty that was visibly behind this almost aggressive appearance. Horrified, we threw the money out of the car and urged the driver to continue. As long as I drink this tea, I will think about it and also about the fact that these workers are probably exploited, although they have a beautiful profession in the wild. But they are totally frustrated and have forgotten their dignity. And also what nonsense on our part to go so far away to another world.

2. Kampenwand

The Kampenwand is one of Munich's local mountains, so you have to have been there if you live here. My way up there, however, took place more than forty years later than the tour on the Roen just described. In old age, tours are recommended where you can take the cable car on the way back, so also now from Aschau, from where you need almost three hours to reach the summit and are back down in a quarter of an hour. The thing is no longer so romantic, because nowadays leisure efforts are popular, and so you can hardly get a seat at the top on the terrace of the summit restaurant. There is also nowhere to find a place to meditate. For this you wear special shoes and clothes and also support yourself with specially created sticks. Can't you do everything in simple sneakers?[6]

But in the meantime I can fall back on a large amount of 'pass-words', as I now call my proclamations from the unconscious. I call them that because they are identity words, which have to do with the imaginary-symbolic complex in the unconscious that makes us do and think so many things without knowing why. One of the best of these pass-words that came to me was, "Say your maiden name." At first, this probably sounds quite strange to a man. But that there can be such a thing at all, that 'it' (or

---

[6] In fact, when I was climbing the mountain so shod, a hiker loudly scolded me for the lack of real mountain boots. Schoolmaster, obsessive neurotic, I scolded back.

better Id, the Freudian Id) actually speaks in you, is quite amazing. Now I can easily refer here again to the Other, who is after all the hoard of the signifiers, of the speech units. Moreover, the unconscious truth is just not the usual, generally communicated and consciously known truth. Also in the antiquity the unconscious spoke completely mysteriously as it is handed down from the Delphic oracle.

But with modern methods - like the analytic-cathartic meditation I developed - one can filter out all too speculative and enigmatic statements. Moreover, perhaps a little psychoanalytic knowledge is needed to translate such an identity or passport word into printable text, which was not too difficult in the case of the saying with the 'maiden name'. It should probably be about the feminine in myself and also about giving a name to the feminine desire. Freud had tried this in vain. One of the first psycho-analysts who corresponded with Freud about this was, interestingly enough, the Indian G. Bose.

He developed, in opposition to Freud's definition of the Oedipus complex, the complex of "opposite wishes" or affects. For example, he contrasted the boy's castration anxiety with the "unconscious desire to be a woman" and the so-called Freudian 'penis envy' of the woman with the "unconscious desire to want be a man." These unconscious strivings then had to be made conscious to the patient by the therapist and reconciled with the external situation. So my 'maiden name' - more or less, I thought - had something to do with that, although in my case it was not about the transsexual background, but rather about something too heterosexual.

In fact, we find something comparable in Indian yoga in the emphasis on guru 'bhakti' (merging love) and also in Western mysticism in union with Christ. Devotion and receptivity were to be developed to the point of no-go in these mystical procedures, which meant nothing other than emphasizing a feminine structure in meditation. However, Bose's theory did not prevail in practice. Indeed, Bose suggested to some patients this unconscious desire "to be a woman" with stressed prompts to imagine it repeatedly in the imagination. The gap between the signifiers, the comprehensive entities 'man' and 'woman' is too great for this to be accomplished simply by suggestion or brief analysis. These manipulations degraded its scientificity.

However, the idea of 'opposite' drive powers, as described, is not fundamentally wrong,. And so, my maiden name is nothing superstitious. As astonishing as such a mental expression from the unconscious was, it was nevertheless impressive for me and also applicable. Sweepingly said, it was immediately clear to me that it was about the 'female side' in me, which I had obviously neglected. No therapist could have conveyed this to me in a more mocking, smug but also original way. Nothing is as effective as the passport or identity word coming from one's own inner being, which I had given myself - via an unconscious detour. Whoever else would have advised me to pay more attention to my 'feminine side' would not have produced a 'yes thank you' in me. But the almost paradoxical formulation concerning the "Say your maiden name" aroused the interest much more extensively.

So I could also recognize that the 'feminine side' in me would not consist in adopting feminine behaviors, as homosexuals often do. Rather, it would have to be about my way of expressing myself and writing, because it is specifically about 'name', not about being. My first books were peppered with exaggerated factual arguments as male scientists like to do. Now I'm trying a more narrative style, though it hasn't quite turned out feminine yet. However, I should still explain how the meditation I use works and how it brings about these pass-words. I only hint at it briefly here and describe it in further chapters and in .

In the center there are so-called formula-words, which correlate to the pass-words, and which contain in a formulation, in a single writing several meanings, depending on from which letters one reads this - written in a circle. These formula-words are thus scientifically constructed and are repeated purely mentally, thus purely mentally, until they provoke the pass-words in the unconscious according to its similar 'linguistic-crystal'-structure.[7] Thus I also follow Wittgenstein's scheme. The catalog of characters is cut analogously (read at intersections of meanings) and thus finally leads to a dialogue with the unconscious, with the Other in us.

In the small cabins of the Kampenwandbahn, one feels floatingly protected and can thus have this kind of self-talk with the unconscious. If there was no comfortable place to do so on the way up, the slow glide down is ideal for meditation. Self-talk does not mean talking with one's own self, but with the Other, which is made possible by the linguistic and crystalline inversion effect. It is my own Other, the - as the philosopher M. Heidegger would say - 'Jemeinigkeit' (the me-concerning) of the Other in me, my 'Thou-Ego' which has become a kind of absoluteness. This is reminiscent of the philosopher of religion M. Buber, who spoke of the 'I-Id' (identical with the imaginary order) and 'I-Thou' (identical with the symbolic order).

However, Buber's theory ultimately culminates in the creation of an 'eternal You' to which the I-Thou must transform. This cannot be argued for scientifically. But one can make everything a bit more plausible if one takes into account that in natural science one uses a 'lan-

---

[7] A Lacanian term for the combination of the unconscious of word-symbolic (linguistic) and picture-imaginary (crystalline) parts. I also call the two parts an Id Speaks and an Id Rays.

guage' deprived of all reference to a voice, and thus believes to have solved the problem of scientificity. One
separates the voice, which is subjective, from the apparently objective language, and then the voice is reintro-
duced as that of the de-subjectified scientist speaking as
if from the off.[8] Buber's God is also objectified in this
mythical way, he has the priestly, admonishing voice,
which is not as free as that of my unbound pass-words,
like that - one could better follow Buber - of an 'Id-
Thou', of the Other in myself as an intrinsically familiar
and belonging and yet sometimes seemingly alien voice.

It is thus the voice that is the regulative of distancing and
proximity relationship (Wittgenstein's x-axis), of top
down and basal administration (y-axis), and also of sexual partnership (z-axis). It realizes the familial or the
unity understood as culturally set or even intersubjec-
tively beyond the man-woman relationship. It introjects
the soul-body-, the imaginary-symbolic unity, and now it
does not necessarily project the Holy Trinity as Wittgenstein further formulated it, but the fundamental trinity,
the triad.[9] This must also exist in the psychoanalytic
session, even if only the therapist and his client are present. As already mentioned, Freud or Lacan or the scien-

---

[8] Lacan, J., Seminar I. Freuds technische Schriften, Walter
(1980) S. 332

[9] I will show later that what is at stake is the triad of Lacan's -
what he calls Borromean - knot, a knotting of possibilities of
statements.

tific claim of psychoanalysis must also be in the room. To put it simply, it is like in a good marriage: it is never just the two of you, there is always the partner's family involved. The mother-in-law, the brother-in-law, a child or even the couple therapist, i.e. a third partner, is always in bed with you.

3. To Hocheppan

Once again to South Tyrol. The best way to go to Hocheppan is to take the high trail from Matschatsch Castle. The castle still shows old South Tyrolean architectural style. So you can well imagine the former lord of the castle, striding along tall and stolid, the children romping around in costume-like garments, and a clerk coming around the corner hauling wood. The hierarchy of the powerful vineyard owner and his workers, the world of the gnarled mountain farmers and their many children, and the myth of the fiery Andreas Hofer descendants still works. Because the "Bummser" (Bombers) - that's what they called the South Tyrolean lads who blew away the electricity pylons - were still fighting against the Italian domination that had been imposed on them when I first made this trip (again, around 1965, but often even later).

The path from Matschatsch runs first horizontally through a lot of light deciduous forest, then crossing the Furglauer gorge and later over a flowery meadow. It now descends a few well-worn wooden steps, directly under the Grantkofel in the direction of Hocheppan. Here you can meet tourists. Mostly without greetings, as is the case today. In the past, people greeted each other all the time and everyone knew each other. Greeting, talking, telling each other the latest news, palavering and 'Hoamgoarsten' (meeting guests at home without being hosted) was still a constant South Tyrolean rite. Visiting without hospitality, just sitting together and talking to each other, was not a party, but an autochthonous group dynamic, bubbling over, talking 'hoamig', as a goast (guest), but sometimes also ' goarstig (nasty)'.

It was also gossip and small talk. Today, no one knows anymore what was talked about, whether more serious things were discussed and thus social therapy was practiced. But it was probably mainly about the neighbors, local politics, farm economics, weather, a few personal things, conflicts and the children. Modern group dynamics usually don't bring more real exchanges together either. It is nevertheless as if with the last war, seventy years ago, a gale-force wind of significant magnitude swept over the country and the villages, largely destroyed all the old habits, traditionalisms and also the carvings on the house walls and settled modern box houses, hotels, industry and established a few ugly and unimaginative fruit monocultures. No more coziness, but also no longer the dullness of the old days, when the mountain farmers still had to slave hard and had many children only so that they were provided for in old age.

Even if it is more uncaring today, I do not find the highly interesting knowledge we have today and also some of the modern technology unfavorable. I think for example - paradoxically on the way to Hocheppan - of astrophysics. Neutron stars give sound-like signals, as if they could speak, and under our skin, only in extreme miniature distance the different particles of a parallel universe rage around, recognized natural scientists write. Sounds quite crazy and it probably is. But we also go to movies that sound melodramatic and in which crazy emotions always boil up loudly, because you have to squeeze a year-long story into an hour and a half, which sounds just as crazy.

We cannot use the parallel universe anyway yet, its worlds are 'rolled up' in several dimensions up to an almost infinite smallness. Maybe all this is also only questionable, and even Einstein's theory of relativity has after all only little relevance for us earthlings. Nevertheless, for someone who is engaged in contemplative methods, astrophysics is not without importance. It gives a model for this hyperspace 'rolled up' several times in itself, which could also be called so in the meditation, if one feels which infinite space the unconscious represents. This becomes especially noticeable in the unconscious body image. Not only in meditation, but also in dreams, for example, the space in our head expands and lets spacious scenarios become visible in it. However, in dreams there is no horizon, the images appear 'rolled up', curved, while in meditation the space can get a wide-rolled stability in its dimensions. It is what I call the image-real, an implied 'imaginary order'.

The three axes in Wittgenstein's drawing also form a three-dimensional space, which one can imagine rolled out or rolled in, depending on the emphasis of meaning into this or that direction. Proximity and distance often appear so incredibly divergent. Sometimes the distance is near, then again the nearness is not distant enough. So the infinite vastness of the universe is again extremely near by its parallel form (if one wants to stay with these curious findings of astrophysics), and our own thoughts, which emerge from the unconscious directly, even if often indistinctly, seem to come from far away. Although they are, after all, the most primordial of ourselves, they seem to confirm this paradox. Even for the mountain hiker, the destination is still too far away, and sometimes he has the strangely alienating feeling like Mister K. had in Kafka's 'Castle'. The castle seemed so close, but then again serpentines were found that were too cumbersome to walk, and although one could already see the castle well, it was simply hard to reach.

So the dimensions were 'rolled in' just as the 'ultra-reduced' phrases' from the unconscious or my passwords are 'rolled in', interlaced or - as Lacan also says - aligned in logical constrictions (défilés logiques).[10] Help

---

[10] As Lacan points out, the unconscious, as the language of the Other, often seems to use extremely abbreviated, twisted phrases.

can only come from correctly interpreting these 'phrases' that work so logically and yet contortedly out of the unconscious into the conscious. When the 'phrases' become a clear word, a sentence, through the interpretation, this will be relevant for each individual, and they will roll out into the great expanse of clear understanding. Before that, they already have language relevance, but they are not yet verbal, common language. Exactly, it sounds then like the saying 'tea-drunk'. All this knowledge is highly interesting, but is this enough?

At most, I can briefly point out again how my self-therapeutic method works. There must be something spontaneous about it, something that happens as if by itself, even though you sit down and make an effort. Nevertheless, it must not be exhausting. On the one hand, it is about a concentration on the described sound image or inner sound phenomenon by means of which the unconscious is stimulated in its "ultra-reduced phrases" in order to release them, as shown in the example 'tea-drunken'. In the next paragraph I will describe - on the other hand - the concentration on the visual, the body-image field, where the unconscious is brought to a cathartic reaction. These two approaches to the unconscious soul life - the more linguistic sound phenomenon (the word-real, the Id Speaks from footnote 6) and the more body-image phenomenon (the image-real, the Id Rays) - I will present in more detail below. They are the two pillars of the whole.

But what use is all this knowledge? As always, more and more people are slaughtering each other with ever more

modern weapons, and we can do nothing about it. Or
they overeat, fish the oceans empty and poison the envi-
ronment. Who wants to stay there? So what use is all this
new knowledge? Anyone who has even once taken a
look at today's megacities with tens of millions of people
no longer wants to go there. The bustle, especially in the
big Asian cities, is sometimes picturesque, but hopeless-
ly impoverished, ragged, disenchanted, rushed, confused. Never will any action, official or otherwise, be
able to change this. As an individual, one can only surrender to the general fatalism, which is relieving, flowing into wonderful indifference and deathly familiarity.
The western megacities, on the other hand, are fascinating, but loveless, soulless, cold. But ironically, we have
the parallel universe within us. We only need to question
it, we can occupy ourselves with it for life. The contra-
dictions are crass and hopeful at the same time.

On a visit to Hocheppan fifty years later (2015), there is
no day for 'tea-drunkenness'. The inner courtyard of the
castle is crowded, the small chapel closed because otherwise it would be vandalized. A cheese sandwich and a
small glass of red wine are out of the question. Sitting on
a wall protrusion, one better directs one's gaze inward,
where at first there is nothing to see, but peace emerges.
At some point, memories also appear, the images of the
many squares and streets, people and vehicles, entrances
and halls, steps and beds that one has seen before. But
where? Where was this and where was that? Yes, that
must have been the Villa Borghese and the Piazza del
Populo in Rome, and the steps of the amphitheatre? In

Epidauros or the one in Petra? I must have seen thirty Greco-Roman theatres in my life; I never want to visit another one. The images of remembrance torture rather than satisfy. But it was - obviously - necessary to see them, even if they continue to haunt you.

Because these pictures do so. A street in Portugal or was it one in Turkey ? Where did I go this way ? And beaches, hundreds of beaches. Where was that again ? You have to wait for the images to recede and fade a bit. We all suffer from travelitis today, a modern form of poriomania, mediated by the ever-expanding airline industry. I have some friends who have visited seventy or more countries in this world and yet still need to go further and further out - probably into old age. They flee from themselves, they constantly roll out, they would like to fly to the Andromeda Nebula, just far away, just not to look into themselves. So once again I retreat briefly to an elevated place on the castle wall.

The cloud-like concentration comes again, this time in the horizontal, inward and forward, it clears, thus creates again the slight catharsis, and that is good. Because that stays for a while, and I can set off again, the way back. Better not to look anywhere at all. There is always the same stale world everywhere, which even here, in the small villages, remote in the country, are clean, orderly and yet also so unspecial. You might think I see the world through the eyes of a depressive. But that is not the case. I try to see the world more like an artist, at first in black and white, but after long meditation a tree trunk becomes purple, like Gauguin painted it, or a mountain crimson, like Kirchner.

In any case, it seems to me better to paint them than to see them for real. Here, too, in the villages in the valley, people are traveling somewhere else, they may not belong to those who, as mentioned, have to travel constantly to Asia, to Central America or Africa. But they, too, are mostly on business, egomaniacs, or for distraction. Instead of 'Hoamgoarsten' they do 'Fremdgoarsten' (be guest without hosting in foreign country). But 'Eigen-goarsten' (be a guest to yourself) would be the right thing to do. The native country lies in ourselves!

So the Wittgensteinian 'seeing' is again about the same principle as the meditative listening to thoughts. One must create the world in oneself, i.e. subject-related. It is unbearable the way one sees it without any knowledge. To rummage around in always new homes is just as bleak as to always remain in the same one. Even if now and then a friendly, lovingly smiling person crosses your path, the world is rigid and dead. I walk part of the way, because that way everything can be managed better (a little sweating and panting). I have already talked about the total relaxation due to the beginning, slight exhaustion. The body is thereby a little rearranged, turned around, and feels for moments like strengthened. You then see the world not only with your eyes, but also with your heart, legs and head, or even with your whole body.

At some point, you can no longer distinguish so clearly between inside and outside, and that is why the tree

trunk actually becomes purple and the mountain crimson. The air begins to vibrate, sometimes the vibrational
waves can almost be seen, as if they were the medium on
which everything appears. As in the case of the hearing
of thoughts, there is then also a so-called visualization,
in which the violet tree trunk is just the real one, because
it appears so to the eye, but also the brain or the unconscious colors it so. The soul finds no pleasure in the
compulsion to look into the real world, it loves the deception of the eye into the aesthetically slightly alienat-
ed. In the end, the way back to Eppan does not turn out
to be as wisdom-promoting as expected. I return, already
thinking of the good tea that will be served. It must be
drunk hot, says an old mountaineering rule, even if one
is already warm enough.

My medical and psychoanalytical activities are now a bit
behind. Someday I will write a book about all the particularly complex and often grotesque cases from both pro-
fessions. But what does grotesque mean. Is it abnormal
for someone to kill because they needed to get revenge
on the horrible torturers of the Khmer Rouge? I read that
in a report. In comparison, the explosive murders of
innocent people are much more gruesome nowadays.
And what have we not heard about the atrocities of
World War II. In the Washington Holocaust Museum
(2016), in addition to an exhibition about the Shoah,
there are also pictures and documents about the genocide
of the Tutsis, about the genocide in Dafur, about the
crimes of the Red Kmehr, about the genocide in Bosnia
and about the crimes of the IS in the Middle East. The

ongoing atrocities in Congo are not yet included. A Mongolian patient once told me how his comrades were staked by the Russians during World War II.

He burst into tears at this, fifty years after the war! The Mongols had fought on the German side. One could enumerate millions of horrors, millions of individual fates. Or is death basically only the happy end of all efforts, in that they have hopefully brought one to the great true and one is therefore glad that it no longer continues? Again: I am not depressed, I like to live, but I am not hanging on to life, that is not a contradiction. After all, what else should one want when everything is already solved? Won't killing always remain?

I plead with it for nothing evil. Already Freud, in his correspondence with Einstein, had criticized the latter's exaggerated pacifism and made it clear to him that there will always be war. Perhaps one day killing will be called something else, but it will always exist. I, too, consider myself a pacifist, but when my children were young, I knew I would go berserk if anyone did anything to them. At the same time, I knew that my vindictiveness and my killing phantasm would also result from my own feelings of guilt, because I should have exonerated myself from having protected the children too little from violence. Nothing is worse than having to bear one's own guilt for a terrible event, and nothing is better than then being able to blame it on someone else and being able to punish him as the actual perpetrator. The opposite is true for the sexually abused, who often feel their own guilt for having participated worse and more embarrassing than the perpetrators, even if they are convicted. Thereby he had as a victim no other chance; he was usually helpless, too small and too clueless.

On the way back from Hocheppan you don't have to take the ridge anymore, you go further down past houses and homesteads, of which I already said that they are all neat and well furnished. They all have televisions and computers and a cell phone or two. They are all well fitted into today's spirit of the time, even in rural South Tyrol. German is spoken everywhere, even though this is Italy. Only sometimes do you come across someone who also wears the blue apron, but who, when asked for directions, says, "Non parlo tedesco." Ah, maybe one of the Lega Nord. They live here, but in no way want to lose their Italian identity. Of course, the guy knows German, and I also ask him: "You learned (imparato) both languages (due lingue) in school!"?

South Tyrol has one of the best treaties on autonomy. Bilingual, a lot of self-determination, and it is the most economically successful province in Italy. Today the "Bummser" (bombers) no longer exist. The writer F. Melandri has vividly described the horror of the independence struggles in South Tyrol in the seventies in her book 'Eva Sleeps'. One could recommend to China's head of state this autonomy for Tibet and the territory of the Uyghurs, because there will still be wars further on.

Hocheppan is an early medieval castle and in the mentioned small chapel there are very old frescoes, in which also really movingly the wise and the foolish virgins are shown. As is known, five of them had taken lamps and oil with them, the other five only lamps, when they went to the wedding reception of the king. This arrived late at night, so the foolish ones could not buy any more oil and so they were left out. The Church understands this parable as the example of the righteous and the sinners. But in reality it is really sad. You can't leave five girls outside just because they don't have oil or they couldn't buy it in time. The others would have taken care of the lighting. And how was it again, would the king have married all of them or would he have chosen only one? Nothing is known about that. The writers of the Bible probably did not know their "maiden name"! Most tourists, however, see - if the chapel is open - and know nothing about it.

It is still missing that I report more exactly to the work with this condensation in the visual field, to the visual appearance. Also this meditative field must be visited there, where it lies between Wittgensteins top down- and basal administration in the middle. Basically it is sufficient for this that one concentrates - as in almost all meditations - on the darkness which arises inwardly in one with completely or half closed eyes. In order to make this process clearly justified, I use formulations taken from psychoanalysis, which are on the edge - or already beyond - the normally linguistic (and just also pictorial). Again, it is as if a something or someone, a nobody or an omen, wants to show something, to give something absolutely to see. And the important thing is that no oil lamps, no light is needed. The illumination, which comes by itself through the visual appearance, is not a physical brightness, but one in the body image, which can also be a body-related cathartic 'trickling through'.[11]

It is a nonsense to believe that one must have something like visions in a meditation. Or at least pictorial impressions. Many notice that the inner space widens and reminds them of the starry sky, of that feeling of limitlessness and incredible distance. They then 'see' stars and call this experience the 'astral'. But this is a detour and a bogging down in the figurative. Psychoanalytically, the 'astral' is a type of transference (eidetic or archaic transference) that must be resolved.[12] It is enough to perceive one's own body image only in its reflection point, as the pictorial concentrate of one's own body - or should one better say as the inner feeling, the 'inner touch', the coenaesthetic (a deepened self-perception)?[13] The adepts of esoteric methods then speculate with the psychic meaning of individual colors. But to what end? The body-

---

[11] Dolto, F., Das unbewusste Bild des Körpers (the unconscious image of the body), Quadriga (1999)

[12] In psychoanalysis, the patient transfers inadequate meanings from past or other relationships to the therapist, who must interpret and thus resolve them.

[13] One must imagine that the cerebrum is a concave mirror, whose rays meet approximately at the level of the intersection of the ocular nerves. Mystics used to speak of the 'third eye', but this is nonsensical. It has nothing to do with the eye. It is rather a matter of a 'second look', of the visual appearance, which can also be experienced body-related as a 'trickling feeling', as an 'inner touch'. More is not necessary.

related catharsis, the 'inner touch' is sufficient, if it is recorded in a scientifically secured framework.

Even in psychoanalytical dream interpretation, one does not refer so much to the pictorial, but more to what is said in the dream or what the dreamer contributes in associations to it. Also the painter tries to say something and not only to show something. Cézanne in particular started this and spoke of 'truth in painting'. In meditating, too, one must encounter and pass through the subjective character of the gaze. One must reach its other side, where the gaze is essentially catharsis, geometry of relaxation, lines of liberation, renewal of the body-image, of the image-real from where the word-real can also be related.

Astral worlds', memory images, visions are therefore not necessary. The light-like or the 'trickling through' of the body-image, the penetration of the point of reflection, is sufficient. It has a kinship to the trickling through in a moving piece of music, and also ideas of topologically winding through surfaces or artistic representation can contribute just as much to experiencing oneself body-image-wise. Whatever a painter represents, his picture always contains a second representation, something semantic, demiurgical, mathematical, which is why the painter C. Matta spoke of the 'mathematic sensibility' of his pictures, of a felt calculation. The Id Rays and Speaks must always be brought into a successful, mature, psychically 'object-related' merging.

4. Madeira

Madeira is especially known for its levada walks. Leva-das are masonry water channels, long, narrow aqueducts laid relatively horizontally around the ridges, along which one can walk without much effort. But in the northeast of the island, there is an elongated karstic area that juts out a few kilometers into the sea and promises more challenging hiking. A stony, often stepped path, up some hills and down again, at the end a platform from which you can see to the last tip of this area. There and back a good three hours, in between again and again views of fascinating cliffs, vertically sloping walls, which are surrounded below by the blue, sprayy water. In the north of Gran Canaria and at the Cliffs of Moher in Ireland, and certainly in a hundred places elsewhere, similar impressive phenomena can be seen.

There are writers who have described these gigantic rock formations as the forehead of a great archaic thinker emerging from the depths of the sea and have made stu-pidly enthusiastic remarks about them. At the same time, the moment of the massive rocky impression weighing tons is only terribly short. The eye immediately gets used to it, briefly enjoys the view and turns away again. A flash that for a few moments raises the soul to the 'rock in the surf'. One must go on. So here, too, it is mainly the fitness training that counts and the feeling of having made, once again, a rocky hike that fascinates because of its barrenness and also raises in the soul a corresponding simplicity and the appropriate pride of the vertical walls.

Long before I was in Madeira, I dreamed of the springtime there. I had seen pictures of inexpressibly luxuriant blossoms and also imagined that there is hardly any tourism there yet. One is in the middle of the Atlantic, I thought to myself, lonely and remote and sees the world once again as it was in childhood days. Seventy years ago I experienced lush flower meadows, where not only dandelions grew as they do today, but also bellflowers, Adonis roses, primroses, daisies, chicory, ranunculus, cornflowers, horseshoe clover, speedwell and Lythrum salicaria (loosestrife, which I would like to name because of his sounding Latin denomination). Already with the memory of all these colors and names one of these word reflections, which serve the catharsis and the self-interpretation, easily sets up again. But modern Madeira did not really fulfill these dreams of spring and remoteness.

In the middle of the last century, the physician and psychologist Carl Albrecht developed a rationally critical method of self-analysis and practiced it for years in a self-interpreting manner. He practiced the procedure of listening into oneself by switching off everyday thoughts and concentrating on an exclusively word-related concept coming from within.[14] Thus, an already solid whole and also ethically significant word should come from within. At the same time he tried to examine the words coming to him rationally, in order to be able to give them a 'real' and profound valuation in this holistic and ethical direction. This all sounds similar to my own procedure, and yet it is quite different in many respects.

In C. Albrecht's technique of listening inwardly to the mystical word coming from within, that is, a contemplative listening inwardly, one immediately senses that the 'mystically arriving words' are not imposing a really new, real knowledge on him, but that it is a knowledge which he - Freud would say: in the preconscious - already has. The 'mystical' inspirations, in fact, seem like poems that always have something darkly sublime about them, like "Urherz," (primary Heart) or "Oh Stein," (Stone) "Light." Albrecht's words repeat a firm patheticness and also evoke memories of the old German, of something he already knows from somewhere, e.g. from theosophical poetry or religious allusions. He represses

---

[14] Albrecht, C., Das Mystische Wort (The mystic Word), (1951) S. 185

something, he is already too conscious in his knowledge that his "arriving words" will contain something elegant and then he only speaks this out. He lacks the Freudian or even the Socratic Eros, something in him does not dare to make more daring assertions, and so his Daimonion (Socrates inner voice) reads like religious poetry.

A really concrete or even courageous statement, a knowledge from the unconscious that would be new, frightening or apt, because aiming at Plato's 'divine madness' or at something that could be passed on to people as new, revolutionizing, does not come about in Albrecht. It is like with many 'medial' methods, where the medium only gets the message from the preconscious, which is already familiar to him, not really from the unconscious, from the empty darkness, from the Other. Why should a message from the unconscious make use of our ready-made language, is it not more obvious that it sounds incomprehensible at first, and we would have to decipher it first? Nevertheless, Albrecht's attempt was courageous and interesting.

I may continue in his footsteps, trying to be a bit more scientific. My 'tea-drunken' is a bit incomprehensible, but not as paradoxical as the dreams Freud had to interpret and not as pompous and pre-influenced as Albrecht's mysticism. Since I could immediately recognize 'tea-drunken' as my own mental production, I did not have to go to an analyst who would discuss the appropriate interpretation with me. Perhaps he would have interpreted to me that 'tea-drunken' is not far away from the drunkenness of the infant after the mother's breast. But I know that as well, there is certainly a little bit to it, because some small remainder of the mother-imago supposedly always stays with one, since the matrix (mater) of the dream is always accompanied by a psychically split-off memory of her.

With 'drunk' there is a desire behind it, and that is, after all, something different from thirsty, behind which there is a need. The most deeply hidden desire shows itself in the phantasm of fusion, the primal longing for the reunion with the early mother-imago or even the one for the loss of one's own, large body part in the form of the placenta. But a real fusion does not exist anywhere, also metals do not fuse and souls just as little. However, I will still describe something of the life in the dying process which neuroscientists have proved by the fact that still hours after the death determined with the most modern medical methods, brain activities were provable.[15]

For the next day I have planned an extended Levada hike, maybe then I will hear, experience something deeply soul-related. After all, here at least climatically it is already spring, it is already really warm, "the blackbirds have been drinking the sun", as M. Dauthendey poetized it, and "the earth is growing the big wings", which will carry you away and up. It smells of fresh moss, of flowering plants, and of the trouble people went through to build these aqueducts, much like the Romans did with

---

[15] Albrecht, J., Brendler, M., Report in the FAS from 21. 4. 2019, S. 53 about the neurologist N. Sestan.

their aqueducts. Today, one would lay a few pipes or prefabricated parts made of plastic, and the thing would have itself. Sometimes the water channel leads on wet, narrow paths through long tunnels, where it is easy to slip down, like Dante's way into hell.

But in the Middle Ages, hell was not so horrible and gloomy, but looked like you can see it today in pornographic pictures or movies. As an example we can take the Cathedral of Orvieto, where the painter Signorelli depicted the hell as an orgy of dark naked men masturbating and joking with wild, busty women. One of them even has wings, has loaded such a playmate on his back and probably flies with her to a remote place where he can do everything he imagines with her. Obviously Signorelli and his time had not yet read anything about perversions, because then he would have painted hell as a completely lost existence in the social media, incarcerated in his own four walls, and traumatized by the clicking noises.

Aside from those narrow, low Levada tunnels, Madeira is the best-tunneled country there is for road traffic. Where it used to take three days to circumnavigate the island, this can now be done in six hours through about thirty highway tunnels thanks to abundant EU funding. With us years are argued around one to two kilometers long tunnel, too expensively. The resourceful mayor of Funchal managed it in much less time. The romance of the flower island has thus also disappeared, only in Funchal's Jardim Botanico you can still admire it. To revel in its cloying, too many and too bright colors and crowded flowers and plants is perhaps, again, rather kitschy and banal. I remember hiking through the Monteverde rain and cloud forest of Costa Rica. There were almost only shades of green there, dark, light, chrome, olive, emerald and moss green foliage.

Almost only, because all of a sudden a deep red blooming 'Torchwer' appeared or a 'Heliconia', it also dark red. Such a contrast, a single hidden and then suddenly exhibiting red in the midst of green hell, has an inspiring effect. This red has been able to assert itself for millennia against the green dominance of the rampant rainforest plants, which themselves have existed like this for millions of years. In such a moment one involuntarily returns to the jungle within oneself, to one's own early days or spilled images and thoughts, to rise again from there.

Sometimes the deeply hidden or suppressed thoughts - and one should stand by this - are also low-ranking thoughts that one does not like to think about oneself. But more than ever it is necessary to let these thoughts become conscious for a short time, in order to transform them afterwards, with a little psychoanalytic treatment, into the Helicony of better thoughts. Low' thoughts start only with murder, rape or suicide intentions, before that nothing is 'low' (unless it is stupid).

Even more exciting than the red of the Heliconia is the hidden life of the Quetzal in Costa Rica. The parrot-like, fantastically colored bird is the heraldic animal of the country. I knew ornithologists who went to Costa Rica for two weeks specifically because of him and didn't see him. But I was lucky. A couple of Japanese, who are as well known for their photo-technical equipment as a whole film crew, stared gesticulating into the treetops and indeed - a pair of Quetzal was sitting in the upper branches of a tree surrounded by epiphytes. Nice to look at, quite fascinating, but isn't it a bit exaggerated to have to travel thousands of kilometers just to see something that could also be seen in our zoo? In addition to the aforementioned travel addiction, there is also the magical attractor like the Mona Lisa in Paris, the shroud in Turin or the Halong Bay in Vietnam, where so many excursion ships cavort that you can't even see the mountains any-more, which are actually the point. It was and still is essential to look at these attractors, even when it is clear that this little red in the midst of the overriding green is a much bigger attractor.

As for the color theory that appears in the contrast of dark green and purple of the heliconia, I refer again to the In- and Expressionists who used pastel tones and then suddenly put a dominant strong color or even shrill color contrasts next to each other. And in the case of the different red tones of the painter R. Geiger, it cannot be overlooked that it is precisely the red color tones that are very close to each other that trigger a special attraction. Even better, of course, are M. Rothko's almost dirty grayish washed-out rectangles, which are the most medi-tative of all that exists in painting. If you look long enough, the dirt begins to glow.

Due to its enormous development and, of course, due to the ever-increasing tourism (you can't say mass tourism, you are one in these masses yourself) Madeira is no longer an island of true contemplation. The most that can be said is that many people not only come by plane, but every day another cruise ship, a cruise liner, docks here. The people are washed onto the island for a day, then - after three loud roars - they move on again. Far above the capital Funchal there is the beautiful Choupana Hills Hotel, from whose uppermost bungalow you can see the million lights of the city twinkling in the evening. The Levada dos Tornos passes directly through the hotel's lower garden and is the most beautiful, because it is the most comfortable, the longest and the most diverse water walk in terms of vegetation.[16]

With this, I have landed back at the swarming, which I would like to avoid just as much as the flooding by too much incidental information and pictorial impressions. The artist reduces the flood of images in his head by working out his own 'style', a successful code of form and color, and thus recalls it. V. van Gogh's stroke technique, O. Schlemmer's round heads, Kirchner's slightly shrill color methodology allow the artist to be immediately recognized by his works, and he himself does not run the risk of being driven crazy by too many, different techniques and styles. The artist takes a step back as far

---

[16] In this new edition I want to add that the entire hotel complex and surrounding area fell victim to devastating forest fires in 2016.

as this field of the visual, pictorial, is concerned, but he remains strong and emphatically creative with himself. The well-known sociologist Bourdieu also described such a 'style' for the social being of everyone, a personality trait that he called 'habitus'.[17]

In my view, this also applies to Freud's notion of 'primordial repression' or to the diffuse of the body-image, the body-images, and also to the image-real that Rays. Primordial repression or displacement is the first repression, usually also the most effective. Freud also calls it a "psychic anticathexis" (something is passionately displaced). The French psychoanalyst F. Dolto distinguished the dynamic, erotic and basal body image. Thus she comes close to the image of the 'corps morcelée', the 'dismembered body', which corresponds to the effect of these first body images. The 'corps morcelée' is not a real dismembered body, but one in the field of the Id Rays/Speaks.

Initially, the infant experiences itself - largely unconsciously - as earliest psychologically 'fragmented', it can only perceive itself uniformly for moments. This means that the child experiences one body image and the other in a different way and is not yet able to summarize all of them in a uniform manner. It is really still completely three- and multi-part oriented. It would not be able to survive in such a disoriented way, if there would not be a reference person in the mother, who enables the further

---

[17] Bourdieu, P., Die feinen Unterschiede (the fine differences, critique of social judgment), suhrkamp wissenschaft (1987)

development of the child - at least for the time being - in the sense of the inner psychic 'object' (the mother's breast or her gaze, which the psychoanalyst H. Kohut called the 'glow in the mother's eye').

In short, psychoanalysis and meditation are about the same thing. There is this diffuse imaginary-real order in which the child initially finds itself. I.e. it is like in an autistic phase, in which the 'perceptual identity', the image-real prevails and unbearable is earliest repressed. One was identical with a characteristic trait of the mother and could thus anticipate a body mastery that one did not really have yet. One did not yet have a Bourdieuian habitus, one was still neurotic, unconsciously divided within oneself. Only with the emergence of the 'thinking identity', with the linguistic mastery of the world, one could become what some people say: 'they are who they are', Bourdieu's habitus.

By having words with which one can deal linguistically-thoughtfully, one achieves 'thought-identity', symbolically-real order. But also this order, one experiences every day, is not sufficient for itself to be able to live well and truly. One has to go back to the imaginary-real beginnings, what in psychoanalysis and meditation is called regression. But one does not go back completely, only so far that one can apprehend, grasp the earlier, in order to be able to rewrite one's own history with this grasping hand. This is then called progression. Thus a third level of order is reached, which Wittgenstein calls even the 'tria-logical'. How this looks exactly in psychoanalysis and meditation.

5. Bali – Gunung Batur

If you come to Lake Batur from the west on the island of Bali, there is a modest hotel right at the beginning of the lake. In my time, there were only rooms with shared toilets, and the hotelier wheedled you into taking a guide to climb Gunung Batur volcano. The usual guidebooks in book form showed the route, but they described an arduous four-hour climb up the southern flank, with a long stretch of flatland to go. One should also get up at four in the morning to see the sunrise. I believe that the hotel still exists, but in the vicinity there are now, as everywhere else, also the luxury cliques with large pool, bar and rip off.

Somewhere someone described, you can also climb from the east, then it would be only two hours, but there was no exact information. I took for this reason then but a guide and explained the eastern route, which he had not yet gone, but of which he was sure to find. One had to drive to the end of the lake, then, in a dingy but original Bali village turn left to the north. Here the guide proved to be useful already because he kept asking for the way, which had to turn left again and led to the volcano. In fact we found this way, left the car somewhere on the lava scree and hiked up. After less than two hours we were at the top, where a few guys were already standing with bottles of water and coke. But there was also hot tea with some ginger added. This was already very close to 'tea-drunk', because the ginger adds another strengthening note to the usual black tea.

Many offer the ginger without the black tea as a background and just brew a few pieces of ginger in the hot water. This is also not bad, but the right ginger tea invigorates a lot more. Of course, you have to like the spiciness, which is the custom in Asian countries anyway. In addition, it is often claimed that ginger serves or should serve as a natural remedy for all kinds of diseases. However, I believe that the healing effect is supported by the framework of the ceremony, which always plays a major role in tea preparations. A good tea is always drunk only with awareness and devotion. However, I consider ceremonial tea rituals to be compulsive.

From Gunung Batur you can see in the distance - rising proudly - Gunung Agung, the highest volcano in Bali. But it would have been a two to three day trip to climb there. Gunung Batur will do, if you need a summit experience to tell about at home. Two hundred meters to the west a small peak was smoking, so there was no lack of a real volcano feeling. Crazy people go to the Erta Ale in Ethiopia. The pointed lava rock is already troublesome on the approach, the deeply sunken surrounding countryside (Danakil depression) glowing hot, and the area also dangerous because of radical Muslims and bandits. In 2013, five tourists were shot dead. However, the view into the seething mass of the volcano is unique, but on the Gunung Batur is also enough, and one will not be shot.

In the meantime, I am no longer so fond of traveling. I myself have also been guilty of this poriomania. The volcano experience, which one can have with the ascent of the Poás (Costa Rica) or on the Vesuvius, one could get also in the Eifel in the middle of Germany. There you can see stratifications through the volcanic rocks, geological manifolds, geirs and unique geological models. On Poás I was alone and fog blocked the view into the caldera, and on Vesuvius the opposite: hundreds of people, but the view into the crater is not exciting. Again I ask myself: for what do you do all this? The compulsion to climb a volcano may have to do with the sensationalism of how people have died from an eruption. Volcanism is the pleasure of death. This is proven not only by the permanent exhibitions about the sinking of Pompei, but best of all by the story of the philosopher Empedocles, who - to end his life - is said to have thrown himself into Etna.[18]

---

[18] He supposedly lost his faith because he could not imagine a God who could not also hate, but he did not want to live completely without God either. Since he could not resolve this dichotomy, he killed himself in the way described.

Freud considered mountain climbing to be a substitute satisfaction. The climber would have preferred the conquest of a woman, he thinks. But in Bali one looks for the tropical lightness, even if one will no longer enjoy - I become again the whiner of the eternally-strict-better - the nature and erotic experience of the German painter and musician W. Spieß. Spieß made a furor in Bali at the end of the twenties and during the thirties of the last century. The Sultan of Yogyakarta had received him as a great artist. His house in Ubud became the cultural center of the island during this time. Artists, musicians, writers and actors from all over the world were his guests. There were no tourists yet and Bali was still the glamorous dream of all Asia freaks, full of tropical secrets and erotic atmosphere. With the entry into the war and expelled because of his homosexuality, Spieß died in 1942 when the ship that was to take him back to Germany sank.

Spieß has influenced painting and the gamelan music of the Balinese to this day. The twenty years he lived there are like a fairy tale of more than a thousand and one nights. The forests full of exotic fruits, the hills full of green rice terraces, the lightly dressed people full of love mysticism. And that's where we idiots go today, where almost none of it can be seen, felt, and certainly not meditated upon. A little bit of this former flair can still be seen in the jungle overgrown region around Ubud. The coastal resorts, on the other hand, are completely the same from Spain's Benidorm to here. An ambience like a rainforest smelling of dark leafy green seems to be good for entering into contemplative contemplation, but sitting there and meditating for a longer time is rather uncomfortable. Mosquitoes, creepy-crawlies and crawlies can disturb you. That is why the best meditations have always taken place in the desert.

I approach with it the central topic: how one can justify meditation scientifically? I have assigned Wittgenstein's Z-axis, the axis of 'saying', on which the opposition 'male-female' was registered, to science. Now, with 'male-female' one thinks first of all on love, and how should this go together with science? Lacan claims: "A good sexual technique is a primitive science".[19] We certainly do not have to stop there, because if we do, we are not supposed to be talking about a primitive science here, but an elaborated one. Moreover, a sexual technique need have nothing to do with love, and even the vocabulary "good" in the sentence quoted above may obscure the problem of the Z-axis. What one can do, however, is to speak of a 'science subordinated to love'. Usually science is subordinated to factual or conceptual contexts. If, however, particularly subject-related aspects come into play, one has to proceed differently.

An example for this 'science subordinated to love' or the 'science of the subject' are e.g. the early humans like the Neanderthals. We have only a few bones from them and also the genetic pattern is known. But what can we learn from them concerning their life, their way of thinking

---

[19] Lacan, J., Schriften II, Walter (1980) S. 22

and speaking? Much too little says the Neanderthal researcher T. Appleton and therefore thinks that only with 'love' we can understand the Neanderthal. We must love him, every science fails here. We simply have to return to 'love' as an expression of perfect sympathy, curiosity, even identification, in order to feel and recognize even a little bit of these early humans. "We have no reason to exalt ourselves above the Neanderthals," Appleton writes.

"American anthropologist Milford Wolpoff says he sees a Neanderthal every day - when he looks in the mirror."[20] And further: "One has interpreted this statement as a joke. In reality it shows a deep philosophical seriousness, a readiness to meet the Neanderthal with love. . . . The word love is not a paleoanthropological category and sounds suspiciously like esotericism in this context. . . But to meet the Neanderthal man with love is simply to make use of a cognitive kind or possibility of experience, a cognitive way of knowing which has not yet been sufficiently exploited."

Love, in this sense, is the most important signifier which exists for a science which must succeed with few or no objects. For this concept of love is not grasped in terms of a feeling alone. Certainly it is also not to be grasped in delirious 'spiritual' hymns, not in the falling in love, and not in the ethically exalted love of decency or neighbor. If we want to go back to the emergence of man, a great

---

[20] Appleton, T., Why did the Neanderthals disappear? Heyne (1999) p. 30

deal of love is indeed needed as a category of knowledge, as a science subordinated to it. Appleton is right that a category must be introduced here in the manner to which it is entitled in order to do the science of paleoanthropology in the true sense. This cannot be a science merely of scientistic curiosity and reduction to the object, to the sober thing. It must be a science subordinated to the caring curiosity and turnedness to the subject. An intimate vocation. An eventful "saying without bumps, (sans bavures) without scratches, as the French psychoanalyst J. Lacan says. [21]

Already S. Freud did preliminary work here, even if only in a very academic and somewhat wooden and bulky form. He thought that love must be understood as a cohesion or balance between "ego libido and object libido",[22] whereby libido is understood as the psychic joy energy of the eros-life instincts, which can be directed to the ego and also to the objects. So there must be a good mixture between the love for the own ego and the love for the 'objects' (which can also include people in object-like comprehension), even if Freud's definition still comes across as quite abstract and sober. But it is about the attempt to enable also the scientist to utter a word on the subject of love.

In any case, we thus slowly come closer to the 'saying' (even if still with scratches), the Z-axis 'male / female'. Also between male and female one has to choose love as

---

[21] Lacan, J., Seminaire XXI, Lecture from vom 12. 18. 1973

[22] Freud, S., GW, Bd. XII S. 6

a cognitive category - here still in its form as a comprehensive 'saying', how else should one scientifically justify the relation between these two. Psychoanalysis is a good example for this, because it uses the concept of transference-love for its scientific framework. The patient, as already emphasized, transfers aspects and meanings from previous or different relationships to the therapist in a positive, affectionate way.

Although this makes the relationship to the therapist completely inadequate, the therapist must nevertheless muster just as much love in order to listen to everyone with patience and make his own soul available (Lacan thought that he must prostitute himself psychologically, but remain prudish in doing so). Finally, there is no reference to any objective reality, but only two subjects exist, which thus meet like the early man to the paleoanthropologist. Or like an extreme mountaineer meets his mountain, the rock, which is an Other for him, a demon, a congealed god, to which he sacrifices himself if necessary. It is always about the same paradox.

6. Tiger's Nest

To travel to Bhutan is already very inconvenient and unusual. Nevertheless, it is the only country that is still worth visiting in my opinion. The country woke up from its medieval dream only fifty years ago and has not yet been completely caught up by the horrors of modernity. It is sparsely populated and still loves its Tibetan Buddhist religion, its monks, its monasteries, Dzongs (fortresses) and Chortens. And it still loves its king, although he (or rather his father) forced his people to introduce parliamentary democracy against the will of most of the people there. It consists almost entirely of mountainous terrain and very narrow valleys, so that people generally live at the middle altitudes of 1500 to 3000 meters.

The Tibetan guru Rimpoche is said to have meditated in the eighth century on a rocky outcrop seven hundred meters above the Paro Valley and thus at the altitude of over three thousand meters.[23] Such a thing must have been really still a great occurrence, rising above the ordinary events (in modern terms: above the everyday psychology). Not only is the view from up there magnificent, but the phenomenon of being stuck to the huge rock face, which can easily rival El Capitan in the USA, must have seemed awesome. Around 1600 again from Tibet came a saint, Shabdrung Namgyal, who is consid-

---

[23] The valley in which Paro, the second largest city and the most difficult airport to fly to in Bhutan, is located.

ered the unifier of modern Bhutan and had the Tiger's Nest Monastery built there on the rock.

Shabdrung Namgyal was the first to create unified state structures in Bhutan and built an incredible number of monasteries and Dzongs. He died undetected by the public in one of these monumental buildings. His death was concealed from the people for decades so as not to endanger stability in the empire. Other monks took over the government unrevealed. The tour up to the Tiger's Nest and down takes four to five hours. You can see the monastery after more than an hour of ascent from a ridge opposite, where there is also a tea room. Then it goes another hour further up, from where, however, you have to descend again in a step-like manner and then climb up again. If today, in 2015, you still hardly meet tourists in Bhutan, but here, on this tour, there are many that you meet. Because it is a must to go up there, otherwise you should not even go to the country. Unfortunately, there are always such links of may, can, must and should, which admittedly do not apply to everyone, but which one gets along badly.

In my view, Bhutan is not a happy country because it has a happiness minister. It is happy because tradition and modernity, religion and the secular state, rich and poor, heart and mind are still in a largely harmonious union. Instead of the gross social product, one speaks here of the 'Gross National Happiness', the gross happiness product. But I think that happiness comes also from the change that is taking place so gently and yet so quickly right now. The old is still well there and the new is also already a bit up for grabs. So the men wear the kilt-like traditional national dress of the 'Gho', the women the elongated 'Kira'. At the same time, they talk on their cell phones across the mountains. There are no traffic lights in the whole country, the only one introduced in the capital Thimpu has been abolished.

In any case, this is not what is often said by Western tourists about the so-called Third World, namely that they are "poor but happy". Such a statement only shows false pity or proves an envious error. The Bhutanese are happy and at the same time not poor. This is largely due to the fact that, as a relic of matriarchal times, women own the land. This gives them security and strength. They thus make something of their maiden name. And the religion is still strong, alive, close to the people. So you have to go up to the tiger's nest, even if you don't meet the essence of happiness there as you once did.

So you have to go to the Acropolis in Athens, to Tower Bridge in London, and to the Fontana di Trevi and the Spanish Steps in Rome, although it would make much more sense to look at Michelangelo's statue of Moses in the inconspicuous church of San Pietro in Vincoli. The body-styled power prophet with the tablets of the law almost slipping out of his hand is horned like a devil, but the horns have been interpreted as holy rays. Why? He was one of those 'mischievous guys' who committed a murder and then walked the 'iron trail' through the Sinai. There he encountered his father conflict, the conflict with the paternal metaphor (namely what it really means to be a father in the full sense), and which ended with the rather rude rules of strict monotheism on two heavy slabs of stone.[24]

Anyway, Shabdrung also does it, the so highly sacred venerated one is supposed to have brought with a trick a relic of Buddha into his possession or to have kept this illegally, by letting the original slip in the sleeve of his 'Gho' at the moment of the handing over and handed over only the copy of the relic, mischievous, slithering. Anyway, besides Shabdrung, Buddha is such an omnipresent strongman in Bhutan, to whom everyone aspires in the form of patient, hard and pious life in the mountains, even if one already has quite a few asphalted roads and there are four or five particularly expensive hotels.

---

[24] With the conflict concerning the 'father metaphor' I refer with Moses to his 'tripartiteness' concerning the origin from the tribe of Levi, taking a son position with the Pharaoh and finally his function as son-in-law of a Medianite priest. This 'tripartiteness' produced a tension, which Moses could solve only in the finding of the all unifying divine Primal Father. According to Wittgenstein, this would be the 'projected' form of finding unity. It has lasted as a Jewish belief for a long time.

All that is a measure to keep backpackers back. Also you have to spend 250 dollars every day.

And also the names of the German soccer players (e.g. Schweinsteiger) are known here by almost everyone, although the country is otherwise still well shielded. Modernity has already moved into Bhutan, this country with many seven-thousand-meter peaks, and so I meditated not on a rocky outcrop, but at a very unusual spot near the village road in Mongar, where something happened to me again like on the way from Roen back to Tramin. I was sitting on a bench far away from one of those big prayer wheels that you have to turn with some force, after which they not only send the prayers to heaven, but also make a gong-like sound with each turn.

Perhaps it was these sounds coming from far away that animates me, but I was absorbed in my own inward listening and suddenly heard once again such an 'ultra-reduced sentence': "Pay differently". What does that mean? One can interpret many things into it: pay differently than usual, pay with counterfeit money for example, or pay something different and not always the same. But it was immediately quite clear for me that I should not really pay something differently, but that it should be about numbers, which are to be counted differently than the numbers, which we usually use. Until today there is no empirical theory of the first integers. In the beginning there were only one, two and many with the people. If a shepherd had to count his sheep, he put so-called number stones in his pocket, a small stone for each sheep. When he brought the animals back home, he could count them on it.

The mathematician Kronacher therefore also said: 'Man invented mathematics, but God made the numbers'. That is a nice story, but for such an important science as mathematics actually too little. Therefore it was not surprising to me that there must be 'the different-numbers'. Lacan had already described them from psychoanalysis. He said: 'A one represents a zero for another one'. I assume that he started from the therapeutic situation, according to which the analyst and his patient are each first of all a one, which counts, but outwardly does not yet represent this quantity mathematically clearly. They are strangers to each other and engage in a mutual language game, an intersubjective speech duel, in a two-people symbolism, and must assume that each counts the same amount, but initially represents only a blank space, a zero, for the other. Only when one comes closer to the other in a complex way, associates, interprets, dreams and confesses a lot, one will be able to evaluate each other and really count.

So this is how another kind of mathematics comes about, culminating in the fact that both therapist and patient arrive at a one, a unity that also represents one for the other. They have definitely stepped out, worked out, measured out the zero-one distance of Wittgenstein's axes, and met somewhere in the middle where they are not only equal in value, but can also count on themselves and reckon with themselves. Maybe this is how the 'number different' comes into being. Mathematicians do not think much of it. They believe firmly in it - like the physicists concerning the all-embracing theory - to find the big 'unifying theory of mathematics'.

Whereas physicists are concerned with the connection of relativity theory (theory of the very large) with quantum mechanics (theory of the very small), mathematics is concerned with the connection of number theory with something like harmonic analysis.[25] But neither physicists nor mathematicians are really getting anywhere here. I only remember the solution of Fermat's conjecture, for which the mathematician A. Wiles needed many years to prove it, and even then many professional colleagues could not follow the proof.

I have already experienced references to mathematics several times in meditation, mostly unclear and not further usable. When I worked in psychiatry at the beginning of my education, I also had such an 'different-numbers'-experience. A patient explained to me that 1 + 1 equals only 1, while the solution of 1 x 1 is 2. I knew immediately that there was no point in explaining 'normal' mathematics to her, so I tried to follow her psycho-analytically and said something like: If two people join together just like that, that is, without real participation, each remains as a one, they do not really add up. But if

---

[25] Statement of the mathematician Frenkel, E., in an interview of the ZEIT of 5. 2. 15, p. 32. I have already made remarks about the number theory. The harmonic analysis concerns, simplified, the 'study of wave-shaped signals', in order to connect mathematics with physics.

they take multiples of each other, if they conjugate, they will be a real couple, that is, the full, the round two.

The patient agreed with me. She had made her calculation - so I could discuss with colleagues at that time - probably on the basis of Freud's sexual theory. There it 'counts' only if one admits that one desires, that one has a desire, a libidinous striving, even if one does not know at all what it is directed toward or what it strives for. The question about what really counts, what counts as unconscious desire, is not expressed backwards as Faust asked Gretchen: 'How do you keep it with religion', he asked, whereas he only wanted to know whether she would also agree to an illegitimate intimate contact. He should have asked: 'What about your desire, do you have a desire for intimate contact with me? Of course, Gretchen would have run away screaming. At that time, one did not have the 'other-numbers', which are not necessarily the correct or accurate numbers, but they are direct, pragmatic and numbers of truth.

The patient in the psychiatric ward could only say directly what was going on inside her. That's why they thought she was crazy, whereas in reality she only counted 'differently'. The 'number differently' is even different, than those, with which we must calculate while shopping, but a connection of both number systems would bring actually a solution for the unification of the mathematics. It would look in such a way that this solution is reached not only within the conventional mathematics, but that one includes the 'other-numbers' there in a system related to the subject. Maybe it could work even better than with the 'harmonic analysis' with the 'perfectoid spaces' of the mathematician P. Scholze, who connected algebra and geometry, thus numbers and objects, by so-called homotopies, thus structure-related similarities.[26]

Maybe that's why I learned the pass-word from the other-numbers, because at that time I was dealing with the problem of dyscalculia. I worked for a year in the neurology department of the Munich University Hospital, where we had to deal with it several times. These sick people find it difficult to deal with simple numbers and quantities, higher mathematics is often more possible for them. Also the assignment of a number word to the corresponding number can be problematic. Thus it has very much to do with the picture-word-real, with early form and space understandings as they also occur in shape and spatial comprehension, as also seen in a similar, different disorder, namely dyslexia. For the dyslexic it needs other letters (left-bellied d and right-bellied b are often confused), for the dyscalculist numbers and 'other-numbers'.

Anyway, after my message from the unconscious and the occupation with the 'other-numbers' I had the feeling to understand the religious life of the Bhutanese better. In the three Buddhist devotions, masses, prayer chants, in which I was allowed to be present, the rhythm, the met-

---

[26] Lecture by P. Scholze, winner of the Fields Medal, in FAZ, 8. 1. 2018.

rics, the sound counting was always the essential thing that I heard. Often the same phrases were repeated umpteen times with a slight swaying of the body. It should be remembered that counting is different in the hereafter than on earth. This is probably so in every religion. Nevertheless, we stubbornly stick to our earthly way of counting and paying, where everyone tries to come up with higher amounts than the other. One day mathematicians will present us with the formula for the unifying theory. It will be a great achievement, but will count only for a few, because the 'other-numbers' for all equally will not exist.

So with rhythms, small drums, prayer wheels, ceremonial trumpets and the melodically repeated 'Om Mani Padme Hum' or other sounds, counting is done differently in Bhutan, and that is fine. When I said to a Bhutanese in a conversation that if you can do as much good as possible, Buddha will give you the rest, my interlocutor agreed with me regarding the conditional sentence. But the rest, he meant, is Nirvana, Buddha is not a giving, taking or otherwise active God. There is no rest for him, he said, he is only the highest example. Great mathematics, I said to him, at least you always include zero in your thinking. That's 'other-number' math. If you have done everything positive you could, there is no need for a God in addition. Yes, he said, we don't need a God.

The experiences, conversations and dialogues in Bhutan were thus already close to the 'trialogue'. These unbelievably high, steep mountains, this fantastic architecture of the large fortresses (the Dzongs also always housed a large temple district) and monasteries and these simple friendly people with their godless and for it all the more intense faith draw one into a contemplative mood. The facades, which are almost everywhere made in the same way with light brownish, dark wood and painted and equipped on it with pastel reddish, yellow green, make a homely impression, and if it comes still beyond that to a differentiated 'saying', the 'trialogic' would be almost reached. However, it does not always and not completely succeed in this way. But one could become 'tea-drunk' from the Bhutanese butter tea - if I may make this purely allegorical remark. The butter tea, at least in Bhutan, is not mixed with rancid butter, as I have always read about the Tibetan butter tea, but with normal butter and thus well drinkable.

Interesting in Bhutan are also the gender roles, the theme 'male-female' on the Z-axis of Wittgenstein, which also has something to do with 'saying' and counting. As I said, Bhutanese women generally own land, but this also ties them to their homesteads and imposes responsibilities on them. In principle, polygamy is allowed in Bhutan, and polyandry also exists for the women. However, it is this privilege that is being used less and less as the men begin to migrate to the cities and adopt the modernity of Western life. So, while it used to be the case that the shoes of the man who was currently in the woman's bedroom had to be left outside the door so that the other - second or third - could see that he was now not in demand, now the modern Bhutanese husband returns from his longer stays away from home for work and has to recover from his exertions. There are no more shoes outside, neither his, nor others.

For those who want to get closer to meditation via external associations, there are exciting trekking paths in Bhutan that lead over the individual five thousand meter passes. The Austrian journalist and tourism consultant M. Uitz describes them wonderfully and also vividly reports about this even more lonely world in the north of the country. He lived there for several years and perhaps fell too much in love with the Tibetan magic medicine that was common there, which always relieved his heart ailment a little. But behind his ailments, there was obviously a more serious heart disease that was undetected.[27]

In my opinion, he suffered from a valvular heart defect, which he should have had treated in his homeland, but he died in Bhutan at the age of 55. Of course, with an alternative medicine so personally devoted and supported by ancient experience, one often feels at ease and does not notice the underlying dangers. If he had not only practiced the landscape and ethnic meditation, but also kept the critical western scientific thinking, he could - in my opinion - have noticed his illness earlier and more clearly. He was too much in love with Bhutan and its beautiful fairy tale world.

---

[27] Uitz, M., Bhutan, Einlass ins Reich des Donnerdrachens (Admission to the Realm of the Thunder Dragon), Picus (2011).

A similarly impressive account was given by Canadian Jamie Zeppa, who worked as a teacher in the mountains and lastly married a Bhutanese man. Very humorously, she tells how it was a matter of course for her husband to accommodate all his family members, often for long periods of time, in the two-room apartment where they later lived in the Thimpu.[28] To be absorbed in the Bhutanese family clan and its warmth, but also its old, strict rules, she finally did not manage. She divorced.

You have to cross Bhutan from east to west, most tour companies only go to the middle of the country to Bumthang and back from there. By chance I was able to experience the dress rehearsal of the monk dances in the Dzong (monastery fortress) of Bumthang, for the main event you would not have been able to get a standing place. The monks danced themselves into a trance, perhaps not into the deepest form of rapture, but at least far enough into the reflection point of catharsis. Between the dancing monks, however, clown- or carnival-like types were wandering around, mockingly maltreating the monks who were seriously whirling around (as compensation for too much austerity?

Or were they the psychoanalysts who brought the monks back down a bit from too much trance?). Such physical efforts would probably be too much, too cumbersome

---

[28] Zeppa, J., Mein Leben in Bhutan. Als Frau im Land der Götter (My Life in Bhutan. As woman in the country of the Gods) (2009)

and too one-sided for us, and psychoanalysts, according to the procedure I have developed, would probably only be needed to a limited extent. The experiences of the monks are more comparable with the meditative procedure I have inaugurated, which I have called Analytical Psychocatharsis (more about it in further chapters).

7. Mariposa Grove

If one is in California, one is almost bound to visit Yosemite Park. Mariposa Grove was added to the already existing Yosemite National Park only in 1906 and has become a popular destination within the National Park. Just past the southern entrance to Yosemite National Park, Mariposa Grove Road branches off to the right from Wawona Road (Highway 41). This leads to the visitor parking area "Mariposa Grove Welcome Plaza" with store and restrooms. From here, a free shuttle bus will take one to the starting point of the hikes. Already during the bus ride one can see the first Giant Sequoias.

Right at the beginning of the walking-trail one can see giant sequoias standing on the side of the trail and as one continues on the trail one will also find the main attraction of this hike through Yosemite Park: the sequoia known as the "Grizzly Giant" is one of the largest in the world at 64 meters! The route is mostly flat, but includes some short climbs with slight to moderate gradients. The Giant Sequoias are an evergreen tree species. They can reach a height of up to 95 meters and a trunk diameter of up to 17 meters.

One can get to know the Mariposa Grove on different hiking trails. One can choose between a short walk or a half-day hike. If one chooses the Grizzly Giant Loop Trail - as in my case - one will see the most Giant Sequoias on a manageable distance. For the Grizzly Giant Loop Trail (3.2 km) one needs about one hour. Here one can see the following outstanding trees: Fallen Monarch, Bachelor, Three Graces, Grizzly Giant and California Tunnel Tree. The whole thing is pure nature and history in one which inspired me to make associations also about human nature because the trees sometimes look so artificial, as if a natural architect had put them there.

Which is better: the artificial being or the natural? Because what has been sold for decades as a radiant idyll, must in reality, in natura, almost and always disappoint. The enormous trees, the pale gray rock faces and the dark green of the high forest virtually challenge idyllophilia. Even if it now comes from a completely different area: as a doctor I saw many people - in natura - if I may repeat this expression again now regarding the view of naked bodies. But the encounters were related to medical endeavors and were hardly suitable for comments on the idyll of nudity. However, this is more difficult in a nudist club. There, naked people stand right next to naked people and pretend to be breezy, joyful, free and completely unconstrained. But this is deceptive, not the slightest eroticism is allowed to arise. It is precisely the most directly presented nudity that demands its annihilation. Only a facade body, a mannequin, a still life, not even a nude is shown in naturism.

Once, when I was at such a place in Corsica, I also noticed that the 'fragrant' women - that's what we as students used to call the women who are called sexy today - retreated far back somewhere on the beach and preferred to put on their bikinis when walking through the area. Such a word as 'sexy' would have brought blushes of shame to our faces back then anyway, and it still doesn't eliminate embarrassment today. R. Barthes aptly asked: "Isn't the most erotic part of the body where the clothes diverge? . . the skin that shines between two parts of the body? . the shine itself seduces, or better yet, the staging of the fading up and down." For it is about "a void captured in the image . . .in perversion there are no erogenous zones . but in nudism there are none either.[29]

However, I don't find inspiring informality in large shopping malls, airports, mass gatherings, and vacationer paradises either. This is perhaps a subjective statement that has nothing to do with what I mean with my scientifically based meditation method announced in the title. But I don't want to give here any non-fiction-like teachings, I want to stay with the if only half-successful essays and try to get away a bit from 'seeing', that is the Y-axis, and write something about the other axes and attributions.

---

[29] Barthes, R., Die Lust am Text (The Pleasure of the Text), Suhrkamp (1974) S. 16 - 18

Yosemite Park is also the site of the rock of El Capitan, famous for its smooth cliff. Again and again climbers fall there, among them also well-known professional climbers. They wanted to break a speed record and risked too much. From the steep east face of the Watzmann in South-Germany, the best expert of all east face routes also fell at the end of the eighties after almost three hundred ascents. Of course: it's always the professionals, the top people, the routiniers who suddenly fall off. Sometimes one can't resist such a mean and sweeping judgment. I have already spoken about the suicidal demon of extreme mountaineers. It is a mystery to me how one climbs there a second or third time, when the main glory is to have made it at all. Probably this phenomenon is based on a confusion of the axes drawn by Wittgenstein.

I always find it terrible, even when traveling, when you have to go back or walk a route the same way or even repeat it. How can you go to the same movie again or read the same book anew!? It is well known that a beautiful marketplace, a wonderful city skyline, a fantastic architecture does not delight the second time as it did at the moment of the first unveiling. But people try again and again and get their disappointments. Disappointment has a secret masochistic pleasure. In any case, I can only recommend walking the Mariposa Grove trail once. I cannot imagine that a second time one will be strongly impressed by the force and size of the Sequoias. Isn't it better to anchor the unique in oneself, so that one can fall back on it once, instead of letting it evaporate by repeatedly taking it in.

In any case, Freud's mountain-hiking complex does not come into play here. There is certainly something to Freud's notion of surrogate gratification, but the converse could just as easily apply. After conquering a woman, one might feel so proud and confident of victory that one can spare oneself a few mountain tours, e.g., the way up the Hochfelln or any other of the Bavarian mountain ranges. But this is a mistake. In any case, I only go up a mountain two or three times a year and then - in addition to a few other sporting activities - I feel fit enough. That's sufficient. Others go all the time and even brag about it, which again clearly points to the Freudian thesis, because he who brags is impotent. If you exercise on average twenty minutes a day, two and a half hours a week, this is fully sufficient. And landscape aesthetics can also be had while sitting.

If the Freudian theory is correct, then here in the problem of the climber, the sexual differentiation actually takes place on the Y-axis. So it is about reaching an above in order to escape the administration of the below. One differentiates oneself as a man on the vertical axis above and leaves the qualification of the power level to the horizontal line. Or is it perhaps about Wittgenstein's X-axis, so that the man feels closeness when he is at the top? Lacan thinks anyway that the act of love always misses the mark somehow, because the man doesn't know what to do after a short time. It is about an illusory relationship that is radiantly bright, but only in appearance. In any case, one is far away from a 'trialogue'.

Again, this all sounds a bit pessimistic, but it is not meant that way. To reach the true 'trialogue' is a high demand, which you may only meet a few times and you don't have to let yourself spoil the mountain hikes because of it. But there are phases in which I think to see, for example, the total artifice and cold cult of ice climbing. A rigidity lies over the whole frozen event, I have the feeling that life freezes, dissolves and is lost, if I watch someone like that any longer. Probably it behaves in such a way that with a lot of meditation the outer life becomes a cramped act, a 'nature mort', a metaphor of the transient and uninteresting.

Now this is probably exaggerated, but not wrong. Every now and then you have to die a little. [30] The game of small children trying their hand at badminton on a large lawn without any chance of success is invigorating and irritatingly beautiful. No stroke that the other can return and yet they keep up this failing game for half an hour. Others hold footballs in their hands, still others play

---

[30] What is meant is going back, falling back, when in psychoanalysis one must reveal everything, unveil everything, or in mediation go into nothingness in order to experience catharsis. This is probably also what the ice climber is looking for with a lot of circumstances and a lot of equipment.

Kubb or Viking chess, tripping over the set-up square timbers themselves. All age groups can be found camped or standing in the same areas under the occasional large shady trees. It is not the scenery that affects me this way or that, it is I myself who feels dead or yet a little alive and imposes it on the scene.

For years I feared sleep because it was taking my life, rested down to five hours to stay awake for meditation. I don't know if it was really necessary. I have not always immersed myself in the good moments of happiness-inducing catharsis; perhaps the sins of adolescence have caused the inhibitions and delays, the pains in my head and back, the disturbing thoughts. Possibly-perhaps I also understood some pass-words too well, because it can happen, of course, that one draws conclusions too hastily or interprets them too positively. It is not always so clear as with the 'maiden name' and with some others, which I will still describe.

That too-good-understanding is disadvantageous can be experienced on many other occasions. Lacan always emphasized that a psychoanalyst who understands too quickly and too well is usually off the mark in what he has to interpret. Also, in his opinion, a speaker should not speak too succinctly and too comprehensibly, because in this way nothing really new can be conveyed or the listeners fall asleep. If, on the other hand, not everything is understood, but one realizes that there is something genuine to what the speaker is saying, one's attention and attentiveness remain focused. But there must really be something to it, because one notices something like that, one hears it out, and if one has not quite understood it, one must read it up or ask for it. Also when meditating, one usually notices quite well what is important and what is not and what one must occupy oneself with longer or can forget it.

I learned to meditate by focusing on an 'inner light' and an 'inner sound'. But this did not turn out to be ideal. As I have already mentioned, it makes more sense to grasp the image of the body, which can of course be indicated by pictorial illumination, but which also announces itself with a 'trickling through', 'shuddering through' and liberating sensation (catharsis). Already Goethe said in the Faust, 'the shuddering is the best part of mankind'. With this he meant the healing return to the experience of the body-image as something that one - atavistically - feels rather than 'sees' similar to the so-called 'goose bumps', as it is attempted with the keyword 'light'.

By atavism are to be understood behaviors or primary-psychic reactions from the very early history of mankind. In the beginning people communicated with skin and hair, they experienced strong feelings not only in the head or in the heart, but with the whole body. An extensive return to these 'abilities' is called a regression, which the subject must reach in psychotherapy, in order to be able to rewrite his history - now in the sense of a progression - by taking up the forces or psycho-physical states again from there. The same, a regression with following progression, happens also in a meditation. There it is closer to the body, especially to the body-images, than in psychoanalysis, where it rather comes to emotional-affective experiences.

Because the body image always straightens up in meditation - even if one lies down - thus representing the Y-axis. One can always experience strong closeness (to oneself) and distance (expanding spatial impressions). And furthermore, the axis of sexual differentiation also comes into play. For contrary to the conventional view that masculine and feminine are determined by anatomy, or at least by slightly different formations in the brain and behavior, the body image in meditation shows little of this. In meditation, the dynamic, basal and erotic aspects of the body image according to F. Dolto, which I have cited, do not appear so separated.[31] They already have a tendency to unification, which can be carried by all three forms, because they flow together in what I have described as 'catharsis' on the one hand, but is also a 'saying' on the other. 'Hearing' and 'saying', as I have described it with the 'tea-drunken'.

Here I could also make a statement about Wittgenstein's 'introjected', 'realized' and 'projected'. The meditation, the 'listening' demands a taking into the inside, an 'introjecting'. But nothing finished is 'introjected', not the too-good-understanding of the sentences, but only their mo-

---

[31] However, there also exists an early mirroring of the self, the psychic "concrete original object" (COO), which is said to be already sexually differentiated (Ferrari, A. B., From the Eclipse of the Body to the Dawn of Thought, London: Free Association Books (2004).

notonized echo, their murmur, which prepares and inter-
nalizes the unity of 'soul, mind and body' - as it was
shown in the image of Wittgenstein.[32]   However, the
preparation, the impulse then helps in the final result. A
very special kind of 'introjecting' takes place in the exercise formulas (formula-words) I recommend for meditation, which I will explain later. They 'introject' only the
structure itself, only the purely f o r m a l, since they are
a borderline case of the linguistic and thus need not be
understood superficially.

The projection is no different. Wittgenstein chooses here
the Christian aspect of the Trinity. The 'tripartite' man
'projects' here the unity into the God presented as One-
ness-One. Another example can be given by music.
Many music connoisseurs, critics, philosophers claim
that one must, should or can 'understand' music. Despite
hundreds of concerts I have heard, I do not know what is
really meant by this. Because of its closeness to affect
and sensuousness, and thus also to high spirits, to feelings of unity, 'understanding' can perhaps only be explained as a projection of one's own 'tripartite unity'.
Such a view does not detract from the music. It just
helps us to be 'tripartite unity' in the moments when it is
heard. Of course, it can be approached with its history,
with the knowledge of the composer's biography, with a

---

[32]Thus, the electric toothbrush that calms children cannot
help the adult, its sound, its 'music' is already too definitive.

physical-neurological tone and sound theory, etc., in addition. Is further 'understanding' still necessary? Is its inspiring-contemplative content not diminished by too much intellect?

Because the answer is oriented to the final, creative, more rhythmically linguistic, while psychoanalysis pays attention to the causal, to the causal of the psychic complexes. The psychoanalyst S. Leikert, in contrast to classical psychoanalysis, has just put 'bodily', 'kinesthetic' - as he calls it - and creative aspects of the unconscious in the foreground.[33] If one wants to bring both together, the answer from the unconscious must be clearly linguistic, but also, pleasurable, cathartic, uplifting, as music is. I admit: meditation makes one see everything increasingly a little more detached. It is a seeing that also includes death, insofar as this is a phase in two sections, as I have already indicated in chapter 4, p. 45. However, I will say more about this in detail only in chapter 20.

---

[33] Leikert, S., Beauty and Conflict, Psychosozial Verlag (2012).

8. Marmolada west ridge

I think the path passed over the Vernel glacier, from where an early friend of mine, her brother and I reached the entrance to the via ferrata on the west side of the Marmolada many, many years ago. It was one of my first real mountain tours, probably without much difficulty, but not without exciting moments for someone who had never climbed up a nevertheless relatively steep and long via ferrata. All this was over fifty years ago and maybe today there are new paths and climbs that are better. In any case, after forty-five meters of ascent on the small iron steps, I was quite queasy. There was a steep downhill on all sides. I began to understand people who are afraid of heights or not free from vertigo. With a little bit trembling legs, panic came up and I thought how I would fall down at any moment now. After all, I had almost fainted as a child and knew the feeling of cold sweat on the forehead and increasing weakness in the legs.

My girlfriend and her brother were real mountaineerers (Bergfexe as they are called in Bavaria) and I wanted to keep up with them in any case. The Freudian thesis of conquering mountain peaks as a substitute satisfaction does not apply, of course, if the woman is already there, even if perhaps not yet completely conquered. But by she was there so double efforts applied. Because with Freud's thesis one must come along only with oneself as a substitute satisfier, here, however, I had to succeed directly also before the living woman. I gripped the holding rope tightly and imagined that I was just going up the stairs to the second floor at home. Slowly, the trembling, panic and queasy feeling subsided, and since then - as already described in the first chapter - I have been climbing each of these rock faces with pleasure. Once I reached the top, the euphoria of having made it was almost gone, but the certainty that I could now master every rocky path, every ridge hike and at every time my girlfriend remained.

I already knew the top of the Marmolada from the usual tour that I and many others did in winter at that time, namely to climb up to the Fedaia lake-reservoir on foot with the shouldered skis, ride the lift a short distance and then walk all the way up again. From what I've heard, there is now also a lift going from the very bottom to the very top, so touring greatness is over. Unfortunately, that's not how it is with avalanches and life-threatening ski slope injuries. The piste racers have increased and mass and risky sports have become fashionable, and so here, too, one has a hard time with the contemplative informality. One has to look for times when the slopes are a bit emptier and where one can then make a few flying turns before looking for a sunny spot off the beaten track.

Yes, when you've been everywhere, you have to remember to be more with yourself. One lives not only in a physical, but also in a 'symbolic universe' as the philosopher F. Cassirer said.[34] Because in the end the spirit speaks through the human being' says Hegel, and so one does not know whether an inwardly heard thought, such a pass-word, identity word or even a true calling comes from within or from outside. The source code is just there and seems to sound through one, personare, personal-making. One can provoke it - as I also already indicated - in the form of formula-words with their broken parts of sentences, counterpoint meanings and irrational letters, as one therapist put it.[35] But it can also be evoked by concentrating on something sonorous or phonetic inside until a pass-word can be heard from the middle of this acoustic. I refer again to explanations in the further text and in the appendix, in which all this is explained again and again simply, what sounds so strange here.

---

[34] Cassierer, F., Versuch über den Menschen (Attempt on the human being), Phil. Library. (1990)
[35] Oudee Dünkelsbühler, U., Zeugnis & Schrift (Testimony & Scripture): B(r)uchstaben (Broken Letters) an der Couch, Les Etats Généraux de la Psychanalyse (2001)

For we are dealing here with a second exercise of the meditative procedure, which I thus call analytic psychocatharsis. In the first one, one had to wait for the - as Lacan calls it - 'ultrasubjective radiance' (the image-real, the Id Rays), which emerges inside, if one sits relaxed long enough and repeats the mentioned formula-words purely mentally within oneself. The second exercise is about the verbal source code, that is, about the also so-called 'ultra-reduced phrases', about the pronouncements (the word-real, the Id Speaks), about the sound that can always be heard inside as this 'personare'(sounding through) without effort. Because in every meditation it is important not to force anything, not to elicit anything, not to be the doer. The two elementary basic instincts are always there.

The nihilistic philosopher E. Cioran liked to speak of the 'delights of death', by which he meant the utter effortlessness, the total passivity and indifference to life and everything connected with it. "For what always have to move, for what to lift a hand or a leg," he moaned again and again, lamenting the far too laborious course of human life. And he was not entirely wrong, the "delights of death" really do exist, but only for those who do not force, create or manipulate them themselves, as Lacan stated. The catharsis and the 'hearing' in meditation is connected with that, that one cannot produce it oneself, but only has to let oneself fall into the inner death, without using conscious, predetermined words or straining oneself emotionally.

It must come from itself, it must not be charisma, but something primordially given, which is not necessarily the material but nevertheless the substantial. Substantial in the sense of the substance which one has to oppose to the 'extended substance' of Aristotle and the 'thinking substance' of Descartes as the 'enjoying substance' of Freud. It could even be the primordial given, in which it is difficult for man to participate, while the gods, but also - as Lacan thinks - the women have easier access to it. The women would not appreciate it, this 'jouissance feminine', so much, even rather call it low and foolishly stick more to the male 'plaisir'. I will come back to this later.

In the middle of this 'enjoyment' surpassing the pleasure, the above-mentioned letters dance and allow that sometimes this, sometimes that pass-word is formed from it. Ultra-reduced', of course. One must not imagine this as the medieval mystic J. Böhme claimed when he spoke of the "signatura rerum", the signs which are imprinted on the things; a myth in which still today many modern esoterics believe. No, nature is not already labeled, so that one only needs to read it. There are only a few places where "the first symbols [here to be equated with the signifiers], the natural symbols, emerged from a certain number of decisive images - from the image of the human body, from the image of a number of clearly visible objects such as the sun, the moon, and some others. And that is what gives human language its weight, its driving force and its emotional vibration."[36]

Maybe we have to go further and say that these initial, decisive images can look a bit different for everyone, because the image of the human body could be special for the child and at first only consist of the breast and the eyes of the mother, which shine like this universal image of the sun or the stars. As mentioned, the psychoanalyst H. Kohut spoke for this reason of the "glow in the mother's eye", in which the child also participates, because precisely this 'shine' is ultrasubjective' (both participate in it). After that, other parts of the body come into play. For some men it remains eternally the maternal-feminine breast and for other people it shows itself in some form and color, in consumer objects, which they occupy with tremendous 'perceptual love' (identity).

It is always about the same thing, word-things that are thing-words, sounds that already produce language. The toneless, soundless, syllableless things do not exist, there are always only the objects 'raised to the dignity of the thing', as Lacan says. A tree is not just a trunk with stems and leaves, it is an umbrella, a lookout tower, a model of majesty, a climbing frame, firewood, ship-wood, housebuilding wood, primeval life, oxygen donor and a thousand other things. It is not for nothing that people used to see a mighty tree spirit in the trunk with branches as arms and leaves as delicate hands, but for us

---

[36] Lacan, J., Seminar II, Walter (1980) S. 388

today this would be silly. The 'dignity of the thing' consists in the fact that in it nothing of a name, a title, a rank badge exists. In other words, above all, and even before that, lies the accordance of the image, which, through its image-real accordance, also already 'speaks' in a somewhat implied way. Image-word-real in one.

These first symbols and these decisive images also become awake in the meditation or one calls them up in this state of contemplation, without doing anything, without compulsion or making. One only recognizes it, however not only intellectually, but originally. One must then add a small pinch of ratio, just as one had to interpret with 'tea-drunken' that it is about a drunkenness that already begins with something like tea, but leads even further. Or which is in relation to a great experience of nature or in meditation as such or somewhere else in the measure of the beginning. Because the On-Set is a kind of faithfulness to oneself, a Set that one has made On with oneself and continues to make.

Here is now an opportunity to return to my promise of earlier and to comment on the notion of Wittgenstein's 'realized'. Wittgenstein sees a certain unity 'realized' in the familial trinity of man, woman, and child. I write 'certain' because hardly anyone will be convinced that the unity of man is realized ideal through the family and only from there. It is only one example of many and not the realization par excellence. The child gives the relationship between man and woman, father and mother, a certain reference to reality, which as family satisfies the Wittgensteinian concept of unity, while the sexual alone obviously does not realize this unity so obviously. As already shown, 'saying' must still play a weighty role here. And nobody has done that sufficiently well yet. Nobody has definitively said and logically written down what the sex relation exactly is.

Now, in mountain hiking, through the landscape and by means of the physical performance, something unified is also 'realized': a repeatable body and nature experience, perhaps especially when it is extensive and always a new hike. I have already criticized the compulsive neurotic uniformity in the case of the Watzmann ascent, even though it can admittedly be no less neurotic if one has to walk new paths again and again. After all, it's not great if you need a different partner every year (even if the comparison is a bit lame). The 'realizing' with regard to a unity is probably not so easy in life in general. There are many 'unity-realizations', but apparently no sustainable, ideal, concrete and well succeeded one. Also not in religion and science, as long as they are only denomination and only accumulation of knowledge.

Remains the meditation. But in it just nothing is really 'realized'. Or is it? The catharsis and the 'hearing' of a pass-word also represent only temporary and - as far as the concrete life is concerned - weak auxiliary realizations. The concrete 'realized' must lie elsewhere in meditation. It lies in the catching, in the interpretation and intellectual reworking of the identity- or pass-words. It lies in each one himself, when he finds in himself the unity of the image-word-real. In order to make this clear and understandable once again, I choose an example which I have already discussed in other books. But it is simple and well comprehensible.

Someone who was very critical of my method, which I recommended to him for therapeutic purposes, but who nevertheless had been practicing it for some time, suddenly had the thought or the inspiration coming as if from afar, or even thought he had heard it: "Nothing said!" But at the same moment, of course, he realized that something had just been said very well, namely the two words "Nothing said!" Just this paradox convinced him that the analytic psychocatartic method, as it has been developed by me, works after all, and moreover he understood now how the unconscious is constructed: namely by psychic anticathexis, by an "other way round" to the conscious. For consciously he had been of the opinion that this therapeutic procedure actually "says nothing", it is humbug, nonsense. That was also the interpretation he immediately gave to this 'ultra-reduced sentence'.

The unconscious, however, at the same moment, slipped him a little revelation, a real and further interpretation: namely, that he had a resistance, that the unconscious was actually saying something 'true', in that it was something of him, inside himself, and yet he also felt as if it had been given to him, an interpreter, a teacher, an Other (or the Other, the anticathexied in him, the inner 'you', the 'Id-You').[37] I refer by the Other (with capitalized O)

---

[37] The philosopher of religion M. Buber spoke of the I-Id and I-Thou as relations of the I to things or other people. In con-

to Lacan, who means by it above all a conceptual knot of meaning, the unconscious center of the human subject, one could almost think he means God. But God is an idealized Other for the psychoanalyst. Freud even said 'God is the ego-ideal of the obsessive neurotic' and J. Joyce lets his protagonist S. Daedalus résonate God as tautological: "God is God and his name is God", finished. God is identical with his name. He is the signifier who needs nothing signified.

But one does not have to express it so apodictically. The normal one is the adapted one, who adapts to the other, who in turn adapts to further others, whereby a large adaptation community is formed. Even if it is very large, however, it is not sufficient to ensure happiness and peace, because other communities, now called alien, are opposed to it. And so, as is well known, there is still no God who would serve all religious communities equally. But the Other (by Lacan mostly only called l'Autre, A) in myself, the conceptual knot of meaning in my unconscious, the big 'Id-Thou' in oneself, can be equally effective in all people. Through a scientific and according to psychoanalytical criteria created analytic-cathartic procedure, one can be trained to it.

Just as my test person experienced (heard) the actual 'saying' through the "nothing said", it is namely com-

---

trast to this he defined God as the 'eternal Thou'. Without using this exaggeration, however, one could also speak of the 'Id-Thou' by understanding the Other as the original 'Thou' of the unconscious.

pletely different than if he had had the conscious idea with himself after some time of critical doubting and purely 'directed' thinking: oh, maybe there is at last something to this procedure. He would have been only very weakly convinced by this external logic and would not have let himself be dissuaded from thinking the whole thing a hoax. But when this comes to him as if from deep within, as if strange from within, and yet exactly like a thought of his own, the conviction is a different one. Suddenly, out of the "universal murmur", out of the sounds, murmurs of the exercise formulas he had practiced, the unconscious had emerged as if audible. This produces cognition and liberation.[38]

The exercise formulas (formula-words) are namely so disparate, so multilayered built up that they not only span an isolated area of life. They are even so multilayered that the above mentioned practitioner meant: all nonsense, garbage. As long as no pass-word is found out by the exercises, one remains subjected to an association meaning carousel, which can be actually also nonsensical, until the last interpretation is found, which does justice to all aspects. And something paradoxical is particularly impressive here. Exercise formula and password have the same linguistic-crystalline structure.

---

[38] The universal murmur is that which speaks in the unconscious. I will explain in later chapters what is the essence of these exercise formulas created according to scientific criteria.

The whole thing also recalls the story of the 'Cretan who said that all Cretans lie'. Many philosophers have racked their brains over this. The thing is not so paradoxical, because in everyday life everyone will quickly think that the Cretan obviously means many of his compatriots, but there are also exceptions like himself. Or: nobody tells the full truth, because this is not possible at all, and so he could also have said: 'The Cretans always tell only half the truth', as he himself does now. Only the 'trialogic' does not lie, It always says the truth, and completely. But one cannot prove this to anyone from the outside. You have to invent a method that infects you internally like the analytic psychocatharsis, but you also have to provide scientific expertise. Both are necessary.

9. Monte Baldo, Italy

In contrast to the west ridge of Marmolada, it is easy to climb Monte Baldo on Lake Garda. Going up by train from Malcesine is not very sporty. To go all the way up is excessive effort. An alternative is to take the smaller train from Prada Alta up a bit. You then go a little further uphill and then take the high trail north as far as you feel like it. The advantage: the railroad is hardly used by anyone, the slopes are covered with bright blue gentian, the view can bathe in it and get lost, spurge flowers, rock carnations, pyramidal dogbane and many other plants included. The path at the top is barren with magnificent views down to Lake Garda, and it is easy to imagine people paragliding down from here.

Something like this would have always been my dream when these things didn't exist. But soon they will become a nightmare, especially when the skies are full of them and maybe motorized flying drones come along for the ride. Apart from all the sports technology freaks, then only the perverts, the rich or the tone-setting, autocratic chief pug will have the real desire. The latter has been strictly examined by the sociology popes Horkheimer / Adorno, and they have determined that he always wins, even if his power, greatness and fame are already on the wane.[39] Even the hero Odysseus - in their opinion - functioned in a similar way, even if he was

---

[39] Horkheimer, M., Adorno, T. W., Dialektik der Aufklärung (Dialectic of Enlightenment), Fischer (1988)

supposed to have served the emerging Greek rationality, and his fight against the Cyclops was only there to show people how the new Greek smarties could triumph over these boorish bumpkins like the one-eyed giant Polyphemus. In doing so, Ulysses makes mean use of the fact that the early peoples still possessed that wonderful quality of not being able to distinguish word from thing as sharply as I just emphasized in the previous chapter. Polyphemus believed that the word 'nobody' does not mean what it contains, but how it sounds, and claimed: "Nobody has blinded me".

As in fairy tales or dreams, things could still speak and vice versa, words still had totally thing-like effect. When Odysseus shouted that his name was 'nobody', the Cyclops still considered it irrelevant, like today the heroes of the East Frisian jokes. He could not draw the intellectual conclusion that his complaint that it 'was Nobody who hurt him' was absurd and not understood. The guy was the non-name and the non-name was the real itself. Mr. Nobody was for Polyphemus the most significant Somebody who managed to appear as an invisible mass, as an over-powerful But-Somebody, as a devilish God. In the opposite sense, namely that they feign clueless-ness, only financial institutions and technology corpora-tions and other VIPs can become effective today.

This brought me back to Lake Garda and to a cafe on a delightful headland near Torri, where I expected a medi-tation ambience. But the small VIP hotel directly at the coastal rock is overpriced, the rooms small, so that it lives probably only from the fact that already some prominent ones stayed here like Marie-Louise of Aus-tria, later wife of Napoleon, tsar Alexander III, the dis-coverer of the nuclear fission Otto Hahn, Winston Churchill, Laurence Olivier, Vivien Leigh. Prince Charles and King Juan Carlos. Yes, if you could see them all there together and hear what Marie-Luise says to L. Olivier and V. Leigh to O. Hahn, that might be interesting. At least more interesting though it would be rather important, they would make the Internet highly ethical and with a lot of love.

Also the tea is not special and so I have to be content with a room of an old spa hotel in the town of Garda, where one has a view to the lake after straight. Basically, as already mentioned, it does not matter which place you choose (I am against the claim that there are magical places), but then you have to be somewhat advanced in the art of letting the unconscious speak. Because unlike the brain, the unconscious does not think, judge and calculate - as Freud said - but it knows! In contrast, the brain knows nothing and it can also say nothing about itself. The brain is Polyphemus, and the unconscious is Ulysses.

Nevertheless, for the well-known philosopher and linguist J. R. Searle the human mind is identical with brain functions. He solves the problem of human 'seeing' and 'saying' simply to the effect that the mind (which is subjective, intentional and conscious) can act on matter, the body, but 'only because this upper level (mind) is caused by and realized in the lower levels (body, matter)'.[40] The unconscious then consists of nothing but complex 'intentional brain networks'. I.e. intentions, more or less semiconscious intentions, are networked neuronally in such a way that they appear unconscious, repressed. That is all.

Because the 'seeing' and 'saying' of Searle permanently liberates itself combinatorially in the still quite indifferent, unclear four letters B.R.A.I.N., he can say all kinds of audacities: that just 'thoughts are brain activities' and that "people know without making observations what they do". Because the brain is omniscient for these researchers - in a certain way like the God in former times. Very often, unfortunately, people do not know what they are doing even if they make observations. The fate of most people in this world shows it to us every day. Are thoughts really nothing else than 'brain activities'? God may be out of date as an ideal combinatorics of 'seeing' and 'saying', but can't we accomplish this differently

---

[40] Searle, J. R., Geist, Hirn und Wissenschaft (Spirit, Brain and Science), Suhrkamp (1986) S. 94

through the human mind? Certainly with brain, but not only with it.

The consciousness scientists, some also call themselves neurophilosophers, are at the moment apparently the winners of this discussion. They say: 'Consciousness is simply an activity pattern of neurons', it is a 'serial, virtual machine', which is interconnected with the parallel machine of the brain.[41] Metzinger has assembled contributions from various philosophers, neuroscientists, and cyberneticists in an 800-page work, none of which, of course, really clarifies what consciousness is. In any case, it is tremendously complex. This complexity prompts neuroscientist T. Nørretranders to describe consciousness as the result of a comprehensive sorting out of information, a mostly deceptive sorting out. Consciousness is depth, experienced as surface', all somehow correct, original statements - but they still do not lead to any conclusion.[42]

My opinion: everybody must have the possibility to become a consciousness-scientist of himself and thus to be

---

[41] Churchland, P. S., The Neurobiology of Consciousness, in Metzinger, Consciousness, Schöningh (1996) p. 474. Now it must be added that for Freud the unconscious is the actual soul, consciousness is only a kind of reflection of perception. Something else is the self or ego consciousness, which is a more complex reflection. An animal has no ego, it would talk about itself like the human child in the third person.

[42] Nørretranders, T., Fühle die Welt (Feel the World, The Science of Consciousness), Rowohlt (1997) p. 414.

able to acquire knowledge about it by himself. The mind in the participant perspective', wrote the philosopher of science H. Hastedt already years ago, 'is methodically prior as subject of knowledge compared to mind and body as objects of knowledge in the observer perspective'.[43] This means that we have to bring science down to the level of general and educated participants, and that this participation is linked to a simultaneous subject-relatedness, self-discovery, self-knowledge. As I said in the last chapter: both, subjective being infected and scientific working through is necessary. Basically, this is the approach that also the psychoanalysis of S. Freud took more than a hundred years ago. He even spoke about lay analysis. Everyone should become a psycho-analyst, that is, be infected by the fascination of the unconscious, and within this framework be able to make scientific statements.

You can also make beautiful walks on the other side of Lake Garda. I think for example of the 'Valle delle Cartiere', the valley of the paper mills. The valley is easy to reach from Maderno. From the parking lot in the lower part, in about ten minutes you can reach a museum located in one of the former paper mills (there are said to have been many such mills there). Here, the production and history of paper since the 15th century is explained in a varied and vivid way. It was only in the fifties of the

---

[43] Hastedt, H., Das Leib-Seele Problem (The Soul-Body Problem), Suhrkamp 1989) S. 291

last century that this mill could no longer compete with modern production. From the museum, a beautiful trail leads further into the valley and along rocky paths to the village of Gaino, from where there is a magnificent view over the lake.

Down, in Gardone, late in the autumn, just before closing in October, there was a good discount at the Grand Hotel, which stretches perhaps two hundred meters along the beach of Lake Garda with terraces and restorations. Here, even at this time of year, there was still a very well heated outdoor swimming pool, which is also not bad for the sportiness to catch up. The hotel still breathes a little old splendor, a little spa hotel nostalgia of nineteen hundred, and under an ancient gnarled tree it was good once not to meditate. One cannot always be contemplative and super relaxed with one's doubles, as the philosopher C. Rosset recommended as an exercise to become more whole in soul.[44] Positive personality, mental-intellectual firmness, good 'object-constancy', are terms of approximation for this idea of the real as psychic wholeness, which nevertheless say nothing about what it is ultimately about.

---

[44] I refer here to the statement of the philosopher C. Rosset, who, like Freud - and yes also Wittgenstein - assumes that man is dichotomous in himself, and that the real (the psychically real), which is whole and unified, only comes to light when one knows its doubles and can agree with them (Rosset, C., Das Reale, Traktat über die Idiotie (The Real, Treatise on Idiocy), Suhrkamp(1988) pp. 50-63)., Suhrkamp (1988)

F.-M. Staemmler, who comes from the Gestalt therapy of the psychotherapist F. Perls, expresses all this much more scientifically and better.[45] He plausibly shows that the Self is something completely unsteady and permeably variable. It has a relationship side and a corporeality side. It is a situational 'process', not a static thing. Then of course the question arises, how one can deal with oneself as such a 'Self' in a correct and truthful way at all, in order to come to its 'Own-Self'. Perhaps one does not have to, because Staemmler writes that this "dialogical self is never completed in its development, indeed in principle could never be completed". Clearly, with the dialogue alone it does not work, Wittgenstein's 'trialogue' is missing.[46]

Staemmler recommends here the concept of consistency, i.e. the coherence, the consistency or compactness of mental attitudes or of 'self-positions'. The term consistency is known from material science and mathematics. The mathematical example I gave above of Lacan and the mentally ill woman may well turn out to be 'consistent' in this sense, even if it does not agree with offi-

---

[45] Staemmler, F.- M., Das dialogische Selbst, Postmodernes Menschenbild und psychotherapeutische Praxis (The dialogic Self, postmodern Image of human and psychotherapeutic practice) Schattauer (2015)

[46] In Staemmler's work there is an empty chair next to the therapist and the client, to whom the client is supposed to speak as a person suggested by him and thus sitting opposite. A chair as a third person in Staemmler's 'trialogue' is funny, but too little for me.

cial mathematics. And so also the 'voices' of the different 'self-positions' in Staemmler's account, even if man here brings out of himself almost contradictory things, can still show consistency, that is, coherence and well roundedness. Nevertheless, Staemmler's argumentation is not quite clear to me.

Indeed, one must ultimately also ask about the consistency of the therapist's 'dialogical self'. This 'changeable, flowing, never fixed and plural, dialogical self', as Staemmler also calls it, is fascinating. But is it not also open to abysses? Doesn't the 'dialogical' here just lack the third, so that it becomes trialogue? Staemmler refers not only to F. Perls but also to general, academic, psychological science. However, he is no friend of psychoanalysis, indeed he is downright an enemy of Freudian science. I try to give consistency in my exercise-formulas, which perfectly overlap with the 'insistence' of the unconscious (the urging of the unconscious letters), in order to arrive - as a third - at the true 'Ex-Sistence'.[47]

Lacan likes to write the word existence in this way, namely as something that is 'Ex', that is from outside, 'Sisting', i.e. constant, which - as it probably also applies to the trialogue - simply exists through the trinity. The consistency is close to the image-real, the imaginary, and

---

[47] Lacan, J., The Urge of the Letter in the Unconscious or Reason since Freud, Writings Vol. II, Walter (1975) p. 15. Lacan understands the ultimate real being as Ex (outside) Sisting (insistend). It cannot be grasped here.

the insistency to the word-real, the symbolic. With this I can again connect to the scheme of the overlapping structures, the 'overlapping' word-pictures, which are equally the essential in the exercise-formulas (formula-words) as in the pass-words. They exist and work only in these pure, formal, crossings, which are imaginary, symbolic, but just also real.

I have shown next to it such a formula-word, It contains 'saying' in the form of an Id (the Freudian Id) that Speaks, so written because it is not a usual speaking, but one that is composed of the mentioned broken letters (B(r)uchstaben). And it also contains 'seeing' in the form of an Id, which Rays as a circle, which is drawn as directly ocular, crystalline entity. In ENS - CIS - NOM the following meanings overlap. If one goes out once from the M above left, then MENS CIS NO, the thought this side, cis from No, starting from the N: NOMEN SCIS, you know the name, from OMEN SCIS N, you know the omen N, from CIS NO, MENS, this side I swim, oh spir-

it, from ENS CIS NOM, the being this side, cis of the name, from C IS NO-MEN S, a hundred this name S, etc. Nonsensical as most of them are, only their scientific use is important. If one has understood them, one can forget the individual meanings, they cannot be brought to a denominator. Only the formal sequence of letters is important.

10. Teide - Tenerife

A Canary Island that has become the winter residence for thousands of seniors from Europe. In the middle of the seventies it was still possible to take the cable car to the top of the Teide without any problems, which was advisable with smaller children, because the tour from the very bottom takes about six to seven hours there and back. At that time, you didn't have to hold a permit to go the last seven hundred meters all the way up. Today you get a time slot where you have to leave, so that not too many people are at the summit at once. Nevertheless, the view over the caldera and the island is fantastic and so is the feeling that you are standing on an elevation of primary rock. You can see over the entire island world of the Canary Islands vacation turmoil.

I do not know if there are still hot tips for a great beach. After all, the south was already unusable in the past because of overcrowding and silent monster buildings. Only at El Medano, where at that time the airport had just been built, there was a still almost lonely beach with great surfing winds (today Punta Hildago?). Beautiful is the stretch from Las Mercedes down to the coast and the heights of Acantilados de la Culata. The Orotava Valley, once considered a homely, always spring-like subtropical paradise, was already unspecial at the time of my visit, except for the botanical garden (flowering banana bushes, lilies, lush strelitzias). But the mistake was probably because I had been so extremely raved about it.

Thank God you are back home in a four and a half hour flight. You can still see a good bit of the Moroccan coastal region below you from the plane, and you can trace with your eye the region you might have been in once as well. Essaouira with its towered harbor wall and ancient medina. In the seventies, the city was a stronghold of the hippies. But first came Jimmy Hendrix and Bob Marley, then painters and writers, and finally the beach party crowd. Then you fly over Safi, almost a big city with its sea castle.

In 1983 occasionally, a fleeing African arrives on one of the Canary Islands, such as Fuerteventura. Now there are a hundred times more. There are only eighty kilometers between the two countries. However, the refugee problem is much more problematic today than it was then. Unfortunately, when I was also once on this island (Fuerteventura), I had to experience how one of these refugees collapsed dead on the beach. It was not known with what he had come over and whether he had been lying there semi-conscious for a long time. Who cares about someone lying on the beach, where everyone is lying there to sunbathe. However, the tourists lie in Fuerteventura most naked in the sand and there are also streams of naked crisscrossing the island, although this - not as described above from Corsica - is a nudist area. I spare the reader further descriptions, because while the Benneton company once advertised with the bodies of old naked people who were beautiful and elegiac, the naked people on Fuerteventura are a bizarre cabinet of curiosities.

Probably the whole thing again serves the Wittgensteinian Z-axis, the loose and free sexual differentiation. But Wittgenstein pleads for moving the sexual differentiation into the psychoanalytical consulting room. There, namely, the childlike eroticism (Eros, as is well known, is always represented as a boy) is transformed into the adult 'aphroditic'. Wittgenstein created this expression in order to make clear that the love life of adults has to orientate itself rather to the Greek goddess Aphrodite, while Eros can only send childish, phallic arrows without knowing why. Now the life of Aphrodite is not exactly the most exemplary either. Already at the prize question, who was the most beautiful woman, she had tricked the goddesses Hera and Athena by promising young Paris the 'beautiful Helena', if he would make her the winner. Later in life she had numerous other lovers besides her husband Hephaistos, the god of fire, such as the god of war Ares, with whom she fathered five children.

From the beautiful young man Adonis, the antique advertising beau, she could preserve, however, only in a small tin a blood or seed drop, concerning which then further myths arose. Today, one would freeze his DNA and make it available worldwide. But what I want to get at is the question whether the concept of 'aphroditism' is really so ideal. In any case, it is not quite suitable for our marital relationship and family ideal. Now, Hera, the 'mack wife', the stiff, stuffy housewife who has everything under control, even if her husband, the mack, is cheating on her behind her back, is certainly not a better role model. And the career icon Athena (the smartass) is also not suitable for the fulfillment of the 'trialogy', for which one needs a figure that could unite the three axes analogously to the three Graces.

God-Father, as he appears later in the monotheistic religions, is another case as a completer of the 'trialogue'. However, he is too much of a mythical 'father-metaphor', the superego that regulates all emotions, and thus probably not so ideally suited to the 'trialogic' either. Wittgenstein recommends instead a threefold 'delivery'. First that of the fetus from the embryo, then that of the infant from the fetus at the real birth. And then the third 'delivery' from the "identifications with the parents in order to grow up to one's own identity. . . With it the human being gains the possibility for interpersonal communication in creative relationship. Through it he becomes ready for a dialogue in which each can discover himself anew in the mirror of the other, and only through this does each become a conscious part of a 'tripartite unity' of human being," writes Wittgenstein.

It all sounds quite good, but how does everyone achieve this final 'delivery' in practice? I could bring a story from Tenerife, which is only a weak allegory to the essence of Wittgenstein's 'delivery', but at least it is quite nice. Namely, a characteristic plant species on Tenerife is the Canary dragon tree (Dracaena draco), one finds a very imposing specimen over four hundred years old near Icod de los Vinos in the northwest area of the island. The interesting thing about this tree is the fact that it belongs to the lily family (asparagus family), is monocotyledonous, has survived since prehistoric times and thus cannot be a tree at all. It does not form annual rings and so the age of the plant at Icod de los Vinos could be much older than previously calculated, namely four hundred years. As the dragon tree lignifies, its trunk can grow thicker and reach a height of twenty meters. When cutting the bark, one can obtain the reddish 'dragon's blood', which the indigenous people, the Guanches, used to mummify the dead and as medicine.

The tree is indeed a beautiful metaphor for the concept of "childbirth" through its constantly forming new shoots, at the breaking off of which its "blood" comes out. How it manages to become such an impressive plant, which also has peculiar flowering periods and thus reaches a tremendous age, is to this day a mystery by which one can study the essence of life. Some things even the botany cannot decode completely and so I see the human 'delivery', as Wittgenstein has it in mind, as something to which the natural science but also the humanities have no last word. I don't need to emphasize it any more that the last word is only carried by everybody himself and he has to make it audible in himself. Everyone must deliver himself in this - according to Nicodemus conversation of the Bible - 'second' birth. The' third delivery' is not only that of the parents, but also that of the own, still immature self.

With this I can come back again to Perls / Staemmler's Gestalt therapy, in which next to therapist and client, as mentioned in footnote 46, there is an empty chair, to which the client is supposed to speak as a person suggested by him and thus sitting opposite him. The therapist comments on this process, then lets the client himself sit on the empty chair, where the client is then also supposed to respond as the suggested person. In this way, 'self' and 'fantasy conversations' are practiced or allowed with the client, so that the various 'voices' of the 'self-positions' can have their say, Staemmler explains. The 'voices' - and here I already sense a clear reference to my pass-words - do not necessarily have to have a verbal or vocal expression, he says.

A 'crossing oneself' can also be understood as an inner voice, it is said. But isn't this again opening the door to all meanings? Staemmler claims that despite the confusion of voices, or perhaps precisely because of it, communication is about "agreement, understanding, and confrontation . . . with others, but also . ... with oneself in the sense of self-regulation is possible." It's all going well with him, but isn't what Lacan emphasizes as most essential missing: that speaking is not so much for exchange and regulation, but for 'unveiling'?

And to 'unveil', according to the Chinese philosopher Tschuang Tse, one must more or less (almost) forget language. He said, 'Oh, if only I knew a person who would forget language, so that I could talk to him!'[48] Only then can you hear the real voice, namely the one that comes directly from the unconscious, because you have forgotten and lost all other voices. And for this one must have a very precise, linguistic tool, and not only the infinitely versatile dialogues, which can also be silliness and nonsense conversations as Staemmler writes. If one wants to talk about dialogue, there must be interfaces in it, where language is always a bit forgotten. In dialogues overlapping one another, one must then further elaborate the interfaces according to psychoanalytic-linguistic criteria in order to achieve the 'trialogue'. I will come back to this again.

---

[48] Billeter, F. J., Das Wirken in den Dingen (The working in things) Matthes & Seitz, p. 60

11. Grand Canyon

I don't know at which point I went down and up the Grand Canyon and also not how far. It wasn't enough to go all the way down to the Colorado River. I guess I would have needed a permit to spend the night down there. But a four to five hour tour was also enough. Hello, hello, you say to all oncoming people and look at the different layers of earth and the great rock panorama. The first navigation of the river almost 150 years ago in wooden rowboats was still a dog-dangerous adventure, because in case of emergency one could not have climbed up the rock walls. But today, you circle once above it in a helicopter, and that does it. The main thing is to have the thing stored and checked off, many tourists say to themselves.

Experiencing nature is a great thing, but at someday there comes a point when even this mighty earth and its almost inexhaustible adventure landscapes no longer provide what you need. Being overwhelmed by first ascents might be an exception. As a first climber, however, I only climbed high in myself, indeed overwhelmed and also as the first. However, I also had to struggle with the problems of the first ascent or first exploration. Once I came so far up in the world of images of the unconscious - or also of the brain, of pure images, glances and reflections, it doesn't matter what you call it - that I felt how one could have problems with coming back.

Even the philosopher Hegel is said to have once felt the temptation to madness. One can understand it, if one searches his immeasurable concept inventories. The Indian yogi Ramakrishna penetrated in another way so high or deep into the worlds of the imagination that one had to bring him consciously again from the outside by massages and awakenings. Such a thing, of course, does not fit into our modern times. It is also a misunderstood kind of meditation. Ramakrishna was much too ill, he had hallucinations and got hives, for example, when a woman touched him. He died early of cancer and his disciple Vivekananda was no different, as if he had magically contracted it from his teacher. It is too delicate to talk about the psychosomatics of cancer, but there are certainly connections between cancer and psyche - especially through the mechanisms of epigenetics.

Besides the Grand Canyon and the Colorado River, Lake Mead and Death Valley, with its forty-plus degree temperatures, are also worth mentioning if you're that far into California. In 1970, the 'Opera House' of dancer Marta Becket stood at Death Valley Junction in the middle of the desert and it is probably still there today. Despite the heat, there was an occasional performance there that she directed herself. Today, as far as I know, the place has become a stomping ground. Thus, after visiting the opera, it might be better to drive to the bizarre erosion landscape of Zabriskie Point, where Antonioni also shot his eponymous film in 1970. All nostalgia, just an impulse to think about the proximity of Live and Death, for which this desert landscape is otherwise well suited.

I have already spoken of the desert as a good psychotherapeutic object of transference. It must have always been so, because the ancient hermits, such as St. Anthony, preferred this empty terrain made majestic by sand drifts. However, St. Anthony was not waiting to return to a nice home with a leather couch, dishwasher, full refrigerator and HDTV. He was at the mercy of the desert, for better or worse, as apparently were many earlier hikers in Death Valley, whose skeletons can allegedly still be seen lying somewhere. The writer Karl May also commented on this when he wrote: 'It was as if a great fire had once raged here, . . or as if here were the entrance to the glowing interior of the earth, which had only recently closed with rock rubble.'

So the desert is too hot here, and elsewhere, as for example in the deserts of the Sahara, nowadays such romatized horror stories and raptures are prevented by vagabond terrorists. They drive out these stupid dreams of the salvation of the soul in the desert from the people already by their bare presence. At the beginning of the new century, brutal hostage-takings by criminals made the news, nothing else is the stories about radical Islamists now. But isn't it really a clear signal against desert tourism and also against too much tourism to third world countries? It's crazy, isn't it, when people from the leather couch and HDTV TV countries just mentioned above fly to those with poor and sick and living on one euro a day just to have a look. I could understand it if they would take all our money already on the arrival at the airport or even worse.

Because we don't bring happiness to the people there. The money we spend there disappears into a few tourism manager channels, and that's it. We can't provide them with meditation either, because that's what they've brought to us. The only thing you can do is write about them. In America, however, things are different. The Americans - not only those in Death Valley and the rest of California - are always nice and courteous to Europeans. If you get used to the fact that you have to pay and leave quickly after eating in a restaurant, everything is okay.[49] They have no knowledge of history, as their nation is only a few hundred years old. I visited some meditation groups in California. They behaved very rapturously and exalted. If they managed to gain emotional height in the immersion, that was enough for them. But it was interesting and yet also communicative and good for learning the English language better.

---

[49] A native American told me this depended on the tip, which was the sole income of the waiters.

But just as no one can be forced into psychoanalysis, no one can be urged to meditate. For most, the reason to meditate is illness, distress, or despair as it was for Tim Parks, who was at least able to alleviate his ailments with it. But his Vipassana meditation means that one has to follow Asian culture and thinking, which he then recognized as a problem in another book.[50] Help can only be offered if meditation is scientifically founded, which does not have to limit its intuitive complexity. Only its methodology must be scientifically founded, everything else is left to the unconscious and the art of interpretation of each individual.

If you travel to this land of the Grand Canyon, you should not forget a visit to Las Vergas. Not only because of the one-armed bandits, as the slot machines are called, or because of Black Jack. A visit to the pool terrace of the Hilton is also good for you. If you are asked at the entrance what you want, you go on resolutely, simply stating a room number. Whether the key hangs on the board or not, you're already at the elevator and on the terrace you get cold wet towels, something to drink and a dip in the balmy pool. My brother-in-law told me this trick. The American with whom I was then talking on the terrace kept muttering something about 'Don't gamble'. He didn't know that there was (in 1970) a West and East Germany.

---

[50] Parks, T., The Art of Sitting Still, Goldmann)2012)

A visit to Monument Valley and to Yosemite Park – about I have just written - is usually well included in a trip from Southern California. Seeing the massive rock formations that have looked down on human dwarfs since time immemorial is again a bit of contemplative wonder and being moved. It is always about something extraordinary that makes you come to your senses. Because most of the time you travel to the places where everybody else travels. On a California tour, by the way, you always go to the Golden Gate Bridge in San Francisco, visit Big Sur and Esalen, San Diego and Tichuana in Mexico.

Big Sur and its hot springs and the Esalen Institute for Psychotherapy and Social Research attracted many artists and scientists. Joan Baez, Paul Tillich, Henry Miller, Fritz Perls, Carl Rogers, Timothy Leary were well-known guests as well as actors. Big Sur festivals also featured Bob Dylan, Bruce Springsteen, Judy Collins, Ravi Shankar, Ali Akbar Khan, George Harrison, Ringo Starr, Airto Moreira, and Donovan, to name a few. In short, all of these were considered Magical Places, which admittedly is not a good description. The longing for special places, for esoteric powers, for mythical pleasures is particularly great nowadays. We don't have to spend much time on food and a roof over our heads, so we look for kicks.

And in short: meditation and psychoanalysis are not contradictory. Just a look at the different methods shows that both concern the same thing and are very similar. They can be well related by their fixed concepts and mental tools: Thus, the analyst listens to his patient with - as Freud called it - "equally suspended attention", while in meditation the practitioner himself has to listen into himself with equally suspended attention as well. In the same way, the "free associations" (the free ideas which the patient has to express in the analysis) correspond to the seemingly free and different meanings in the exercise formulas (formula-words) which I will explain later and further, and also to the appearance of other thoughts in the meditation. But the unspecific thoughts are pushed away in favor of a linguistically founded meaning-knotting of the formula-words. Thus the ideas are already somewhat guided, or purely formally pre-structured.[51]

The analyst is indeed much more personally present during the application of the psychoanalytic procedure (as transference object and as interpreter). I have already pointed out the hindering aspects of countertransference. Also the " equally suspended attention " is problematic. It can never reach as far into the depth as in a meditation, since the therapist must at the same time remain close to the patient. Moreover, no one can really associate as deeply and completely spontaneously as would be good. Nevertheless, the parallels outweigh for both methods.

---

[51] The word "guided" is not contradicted by the fact that in meditation one tries to eliminate "ideas" as much as possible. They can never be completely eliminated and after a time of meditation many thoughts arise again, which can affect the next meditation again.

In meditation, the physical person of the teacher recedes into the background, but the teaching as such is more rigid. Here the transmission takes place, so to speak, into the pure virtual space, into the nothingness. This has always been called this a general, wild transference or transference outside the analysis. However, the "free associations" in meditation are of a different kind. They are divided into the more pictorial aspects that arise spontaneously during meditation and are not so important. In contrast, the associations that the unconscious directly contributes to the pass-word formation are crucial. They are also more authentic and important than those in classical psychoanalysis.

For they come directly from the intersection of still hardly verbal, that is really very unconscious, though symbolically pre-structured parts of the unconscious. They mix with the normal linguistic parts at the moment of the beginning awakening and becoming conscious and thus form the pass-word or identity word. I remind again of Lacan's 'linguistic crystal', which represents just this point of intersection. Nevertheless, in both procedures, in psychoanalysis as well as in meditation, the same basics prevail. They are only differently weighted and have the same result: a dialogue without specifications, that is, a purely intersubjective conversation without a specific reference. Pass-words, which assume a middle position between words in dreams and their interpretation, recognition of unconscious connections, all these are completely parallel processes in both methods. The final reference to the tri-alogue has to be made by everyone himself, if necessary by participating in the expansion and further development of the method.

During the transition from the animal to the human being there must have been a phase of multiple perception, thus of a "difference in the identical", a simultaneous multi-layered image perception, which can thus lead to an "over - perception" or "synchronous perception".[52] This process, which actually takes place in every human being, we usually no longer take conscious notice of, because otherwise we would be driven crazy by the multi-layeredness of the images. As it is popularly said, we perceive "selectively" (and this is also good for everyday life) and verbalize things unconsciously (which is not so good). I'll give a final installment on this topic of image and gaze theory later.

Symbolic and imaginary, word and image, something that Speaks and Rays are connected and knotted intensively in the most original. This can be taken from the psychoanalytic instinct theory (drive to express oneself or speech instinct and drive to perception, visual instinct) as well as from the juxtaposition of the humanities and the natural sciences. When Kant spoke of the 'thing in itself', the 'thing' belonged to the realm of physis, of nature, but the 'in itself' belonged to the realm of spirit, of ideas. For what should that be, a one "in itself"? An 'out-of-itself', an 'in-and-for-itself', something 'as-such' - all mental artifices, as they are usual for philosophy and

---

[52] Lacan, J., Seminar Nr. I, Walter (1980) S. 218

also the other humanities. Ultimately, it is about us as a subject, as a subject that can no longer be objectified or reified from the outside. As such it is grasped precisely in psychoanalysis, but also quite specifically in the method of Analytic Psychocatharsis, in that the ultimate support is the closely combined and purely substantial Id Rays/Speaks belonging purely to 'jouissance'.

12. The Moses Mountain

In front of St. Catherine's Monastery at Sinai, a path on the left leads to Djebel Mussa, the Moses Mountain. It was a mistake to take a camel, because it went slower in the end than if I and my wife had walked relatively briskly. Besides, one was never sure whether the camel would not stumble at the precipice and so we dismissed the camel driver with his animal and the entire payment after only two hundred meters. After about an hour on foot, we arrive at the top of an overgrown plateau, known after the prophet Elijah, where Moses is said to have left his faithful behind to walk alone up the approximately 750 steps to the summit, where he received his stone tablets.

All this is not historically confirmed, but nevertheless one has the feeling of walking an important path. Of course, you are never alone on this tour and there are also many people at the top. To go down, it is recommended to take the path more to the west, which is steeper and consists only of huge steps and is probably used only by a few people. At the same time, it can be shortened in many places by jumps and is in no way boring. Instead of going to the monastery we visited a Bedouin family a bit off and gave away some of our pens. I always take a large number of them with me, because for children, but often also for adults, this is a welcome gift and one gets in good contact. Unfortunately, I don't know enough Arabic and people don't know enough English. But I take an outer photo and an inner picture with me, how the woman bakes a flatbread on an upturned bowl. We get a good piece of it as food for the way and outside, when leaving, we get a small bracelet as a gift from a woman's hand extended out of the tent canvas below.

Ridiculous, these little tourist delights. One should have a better command of the languages of all the countries one travels to, only that would be international under-standing. But now to the nearby Coloured Canyon, which is fantastic and not difficult to hike through, even if you have to slide through a hole in the rock at one point. You must not be overweight or you will get stuck. The canyon is up to forty meters high and about one kilometer long. Of this one must show a necessarily col-or picture.

Such rock walls could almost be suitable for a kind of devotion. Maybe only to get an impulse for it. Because I want to justify and recommend something scientific in this direction, and there I must not come up with too much nature romanticism, beauty spirituality or even religious esotericism. Anyway, I constantly make the mistake of pointing out a contemplative ambience, but then again to evaluate every aesthetic, every magical seeming place as negative. It is not wrong to enjoy the painterly nature or the genius of an artist who - if I may say so simplistically and purely allegorically - shows something moving with a few 'strokes'. Pastel colors always have their charm and there were painters, such as Turner, who consciously painted meditative pictures, where one only had to guess what was meant.

I do not want to deny that mountain hikes just like art, music and other things can stimulate meditation or are even directly a piece of meditation, but on the other hand they do not apply equally to all methods and people. This has not always come out in my descriptions of the hiking trails. However, I want to convey that the actual meditation is the one that is scientifically based and thus precisely not brought about by a language that conveys meaning. The sense has to be created by the meditation first. All religious, nature-based, or mystical forms of meditation are well suited for home use, but not for guaranteeing a clear science of the subject. The subject (not any subjectivity) "is in our time that which as subject defines the existence of science".[53]

---

[53] Lacan, J., An die Psychiater, Vortrag (To the Psychiatrists, ecture) von 10. 11. 1967, Riss (2020)

Only by an immediate going inward it comes about that basically the unconscious is the thinking, because only in this way also the 'hearing of thoughts', the symbolically, word-wise mediating unconscious comes into appearance (pass-words). This is decisively important. For nature, art and especially music do not speak as precisely as a process based on language can. They all can also not tell the truth, which I - in the very last - consider to be the cause of all being. Wittgenstein's 'seeing' and 'hearing' still go together easily, but to integrate 'saying' into it, too, is not so easy.

In classical, conventional psychoanalysis it is the other way round. Here the 'saying' comes decisively to the fore, but one 'sees' and 'hears' nothing in the sense of these Wittgensteinian nomenclatures. One speaks a lot about the so-called 'primal scene', but one does not take a - at least short, fleeting - look into it.[54] That would be too traumatic for psychoanalytic therapy. There have always been authors who have argued for bringing the trauma into the analysis, but either it does not succeed because the analysis operates in too everyday verbal terms or the analyst would have to intervene so crudely that this intervention would itself be traumatic again. The definite,

---

[54] It is about the view into an intimate scene, into erotic-aggressive events of the parents or important reference persons. Often this scene becomes a trauma only later, when one has increasingly recognized what exactly it was about and how closely and deeply one experienced oneself involved in it. The original scene thus always resembles a trauma of abuse.

distinct, symbol-dense word from within can come from the traumatic region, and will not be hurtful if contemplation is assured.

Art, even music, which we experience as intense and emotionally moving, does not say it in such a revealing way. Of course, all these cultural achievements can help us get over traumatic experiences, but not completely and not rationally. If this were the case, Freudian science would not have been needed. It is true that 'saying' in Freud and Wittgenstein is mainly arranged around gender differentiation. But I don't know of any other science that enables such a direct, personal and to the point 'saying'. The term gender or sexual differentiation is perhaps not ideally conceived. Freud's approach to speak of a primordial 'bisexual' disposition in every human being is possibly too sweeping. Not for nothing did Wittgenstein look for a way out, which he believed to be able to expand and improve with the term 'trisexuality'. But honestly, what is that supposed to be?

Male, female and diverse? Lacan already made fun of the fact that J. P. Sartre's female partner, S. de Beauvoir, called her major work 'The Second Sex'. "How can you write about women and call them the second sex? Why not the first sex? Ridiculous!" A laugh is in order for psychoanalysts mainly because they believe that there is only one gender anyway, no matter what you call it. Because one has to approach the matter differently. Namely, there is only one libido, which appears to be active and just a bit more male-oriented. Also women can make this libido their own, but in the sexual area it remains equally determining for all sexes.

That which is intrinsic to the feminine in the very last sense must be called something else. I have already referred to Wittgenstein's 'aphroditism', which he contrasted with the masculine and not overly mature 'eroticism'. Now I already showed above that Aphrodite is also not exactly the best example for this actually feminine and mature erotic. Aphrodite uses quite violently the rather in-fantile male sexual libido. There exists perhaps no woman at all who could give the ideal name for the comprehensively feminine. From Madame de Pompadour to Maria Callas or Marylin Monroe there is none.

The psychoanalyst R. Golan, however, has worked out this identity of the 'female object' (psychoanalytically one calls an inner organization a 'psychic object') particularly well. She calls it the 'jouissance feminine', the 'female enjoyment', which is a different form than the 'phallic', more oriented to the masculine, but paradoxically also represents enjoyment mostly chosen by women. However, the 'jouissance feminine' represents a holistic enjoyment that includes pain and suffering, but instead includes 'universality, boundlessness, height, insight/enlightenment, knowledge, freedom, and bliss.'[55] So this 'female enjoyment' cannot be compared at all with the male, 'phallic' eroticism, even though - as Freud points out - both sexes go through the same 'phallic phase' in their development.

---

[55] Golan, R. Loving Psychoanalysis, Karnak (2006)

So, since both sexes go through or can go through these two positions, there can be masculine women and feminine men, which is really not news now. The problem is only that the women, as already mentioned, do not appreciate and approve of this 'enjoyment', this 'jouissance feminine', which is peculiar to them. Already in the 'phallic phase' they deny it and also themselves, then find in later life only a made-up 'aphroditic', while the men are incapable of making the 'jouissance' their own. They do not find their 'maiden name'. What is necessary, then, does not consist in Wittgenstein's 'trisexuality', for this could only be a reinforcement of the male optic.

What would be necessary is a general access to 'jouissance', which I also call the 'autochthonous enjoyment', namely that, as Lacan writes, nature and animals also possess. "Even the cat enjoys when it purrs" he says. In the end, he even wondered if enjoyment is not a characteristic of the living par excellence, that is, that plants also enjoy,[56] and confirms quite vehemently elsewhere that trees, amoebas, and bacteria also enjoy.[57] Now it is difficult to imagine what all this should mean, but it would be a solution for all the problems in the humanities and natural sciences, what is the last common denominator.

Freud has always been reproached because with the concept of the 'passive libido' he practically imputed or rec-

---

[56] Lacan, J., Lettres de L'Ècole freudienne, Nr. 16 (1975) S. 192

[57] Lacan, J., Seminar XXI, Vortrag vom 23. 4. 1974.

ommended something like a passive masculinity to women. What would be necessary is an autochthonous, original femininity, one with which one can bear to live in a psychically 'fragmented body', to be 'tripartite' with the sure knowledge to find a unity for it in the true 'jouissance', which is also that of the trialogue. To be always able to speak like this in the name of the name of all names is really ideal. It means to be able to listen and to listen again, because in this way one can already hear the beginning of the real name. This name is then to be matched with the names that one has available from oneself as the second (the other within), so that finally the third will be to be 'heard'.

The psychoanalyst R. Golan has referred to the concept of 'female enjoyment' by assuming that the libido - she still wanted to save this concept as superior - is not passive in the woman, but comes full circle in her. It does not immediately penetrate to the outside and thus lets the woman - seen from the libidinous aspect - rest in herself. In the man, on the other hand, the libido strives for an external object, the drive must be satisfied by means of the object in order to return to itself. Of these two processes, overlaps exist in exactly these contexts, which play out in the 'saying' of Wittgenstein's 'trialogue'. It is a 'saying' that must be good, accurate and without 'bavures' (scratches), and of which one must also know correctly. Well said and rightly known is the decisive domain, which I too probably satisfy only too little here.

Certainly it has been said well in former times. Saint Hildegard of Bingen, for example, mentioned that in deep devotion and contemplation as well as on the "Last Day" the "fixed stars" whirl wildly. She did not mean all the stars and galaxies in the pure astrophysical sense and did not think with the 'Last Day' of the 'Big Crash', as the scientists call today the end of the universe in correlation to the 'Big Bang' as its beginning. She has rather thought of something like 'points of light', like an Id Rays, which guarantee the hold, the stability of the world and of the human being just by their fixation. Maybe she has guessed that the universe is billions of light-years big, but she has not really known that.

But she said well that the image-real can take enormous proportions when meditating, so that one can be seriously frightened. Moreover, the saint had such a strong faith that she could endure such phenomena of confusion and therefore write about the immense importance of the swirling 'fixed stars'. Moreover, the saint had such a strong faith that she could endure such phenomena of confusion and therefore write about the immense importance of the swirling 'fixed stars'. Today, since we know this correctly and cannot believe so strongly, we must say it differently. But how, so that it is not only correctly known, but also still well said? It is clear that the rays of the fixed stars, which whirl through each other at death, were held by Saint Hildegard through the speaking of her enormous faith.

Today, and first of all, we must be able to say the saying by means of science, such as psychoanalysis. Here, after all, the emphasis is on 'listening' and 'speaking'.Too much picture, 'star points' or so-called 'astral', is avoided.

With the formula and pass-words I am also on the safe, scientific side in the method inaugurated by me, thus with the 'rightly known'. Secondly, it is about the Rays of the 'catharsis', the 'trickling through' triggered at the body image, which results in the certainty of an inner stability with the 'fixed stars' of Saint Hildegard. In the body image, sometimes such effects can occur that almost make one dizzy. But if one concentrates, as already described at the beginning, on the 'visual' and rather to be felt body image in front of oneself, in the horizontal plane in front of one, one will not deviate too far into the pictorial. Above all, the 'hearing' helps here to change immediately to the secured middle position between the 'seeing', the visual field, and the auditory-speaking field. Here still some further 'well said' must be said.

13. In Bregaglia

The Bregaglia is located in Switzerland, it is the valley that leads from Italy to the Maloja Pass. The most charming place in Bergell (German name) is Soglio, which consists of a few small winding streets, houses, huts and the hotel Palazzo Salis. In this old and beautiful building there is also a Rilke room, furnished with the appropriate hundred-year-old furniture. Whether Rilke continued to write his Duino Elegies there, as he did in the Chateau de Muzot a little further away, is not known. In any case, this valley must have been poor and dark for a long time, if one reads the biography of the sculptor and painter A. Giacometti, who came from Stampa, which is already closer to the Maloja Pass. Unpleasant school years accompanied him until he broke off his education and decided to become an artist.

Giacometti's gaunt, exaggeratedly elongated figures are dedicated to surrealism and for me they have always been attempts to show man in his supernatural, 'spiritual' upward striving, in which he did give the vertical the accentuated preference over the social, the communicative horizontal. They are fantastic objects of meditation that pull you up into the infinite. It took enormous courage trying to succeed with something so extraordinary. But he succeeded, his works are in great demand all over the world and his figure 'pointing man' alone achieved 141 million dollars at an auction.

You can walk from Soglio to the Maloja Pass, but the path is not always flat. It goes up and down, and it is enough to get to Casaccia, which is still below the serpentine road at the top of the pass. Besides following the footsteps of Rilke and Giacometti, you can also walk in the footsteps of the painter G. Segantini, who lived here for many years. Finally, I must mention S. Freud, who stayed in the hotel in Maloja with his sister-in-law in room no. 11 (today no. 23). Freud's wife Martha could not be persuaded to travel, so Freud often went on trips with her sister Minna. There were many stories about this.

After all, the private life of the first great psychoanalyst was no small matter. And Freud sometimes had to fight off intense speculation as to whether or not he had had an affair with Minna. But just as with Goethe, of whom it is still not known whether he had intimate contact with Lady von Stein, this will probably never be proven in the case of Freud either. Actually, it does not matter what is really true, if it also mainly pleases the curiosity. In any case, the sociologist F. Maciejewski discovered the entry in the hotel directory at the beginning of the new century (2001) and speculated about the background.[58] And also when walking and climbing, one is glad to think about the old times and these former figures.

Although Bergell feels friendly and warm in summer, in winter - locked in high mountain and rock walls - it must have been very dark, cold and a bit gloomy. Or at least it was, because today there is also enough tourism there, because hiking in Bergell has become very fashionable. After all, this is still the most harmless kind of exotic-cultic vacation. Mountain biking in Tibet, trekking in the Drakensberg mountains of South Africa or on the Mut-wanga route in Zaire, diving in East Timor and kayaking around South America offer much more - because why should you do all this only in Europe. At some point, this will become quite bizarre to everyone, and you might just go back to jogging on your doorstep.

Because one misses nothing. No, nothing is as exciting as having the feeling that one is on the trail of the truth as the very important existential and the enjoyment as the substantial. The I may be a wavering 'imaginary object', but Id, the subject, that which is subordinate to the unconscious, to the essential, has the highest priority and explosiveness in all world events. For it prevents one from getting too involved in the intricacies of the world, in which there is constant gunfire, action drama, and pseudo-melancholy, not only on television, if one ventures too far. But the filmmakers juggle with their Ego's,

---

[58] Maciejewski, F., Freud in Maloja, Osburg Verlag (2008)

they say they have to portray the most curious, morbid and upsetting relationship stories, otherwise the hatred doesn't come out properly, the anger only too meekly, and the sex doesn't come out glaringly enough, because that's what it is exclusively!

To drive back from Bergell over the Splügen pass is a special attraction. Hardly anyone drives this route because the way over St. Moritz is the easier one. Admittedly, the road over Lake Sils and Silvaplana is perhaps even more charming, but rather not recommended in the times of high season. What is worth seeing, however, is a not too far detour to the Parco Nationale del Val Grande on Lake Maggiore. This is a very extensive mountainous area between Lake Maggiore and Switzerland.

Interestingly, hardly any tourists come there, because already the road over the Strada Cicogna from Verbania is so narrow that you would not pass any oncoming vehicle even on longer stretches. After about half an hour of driving on this road, you end up in the middle of the park in Cicogna and park your vehicle there. Cicogna itself consists of only a few houses, but interesting and beautiful is the one and a half hour hike through the valley with raging river and deciduous forest to Pogallo. This path through difficult terrain is at times so well built with slabs, steps and bridges that you wonder. But after about one and three quarters hours you reach a magnificent plateau and learn that you were traveling on the 'Strada Sutermeister', a former transport route.

A small hamlet comes into view, consisting of a few low-rise granite houses in which no one seems to live. It is only later, when reading up at home, that one learns that it was here, in 1874, that the Swiss C. Sutermeister went into the timber business in a big way, built the path for timber transport and constructed several buildings and an electric timber transport cableway. An author at mountainzones.com writes that Sutermeister "was a kind of "universal genius" who not only built Italy's first hydroelectric power plant at Cossogno, founded a shipping company, participated in the founding of the Banca Populare di Intra, founded the Sezione Verbano Intra of the Italian Alpine Club with a friend in 1874, and fathered 12 children with his wife Carolina along the way." Sutermeister's wood was shipped as far as Milan.

But that is not all that needs to be told about Pogallo. Bad things happened in 1944 after partisans attacked an Italian Fascist quarter and took refuge in the National Park, Germans and Italians then carried out a revenge campaign and ransacked the whole Val Grande. 460 partisans and over 200 soldiers died. You can read about it on a plaque at the edge of the large meadow. The ruins of Sutermeister's mansion, the stone huts, which are supposedly taken care of by the "Amici di Pogallo", and the memorial plaque with pictures, all together make you curious and - even more - thoughtful about former lives.

It is hard to imagine that the war raged even in such an extremely remote area. There are also written accounts of how desperately a mother begged for the life of her son, who survived the massacre but was nevertheless executed shortly before the end of the war. This kind of thing also happened in Germany itself on many occasions. Although the Americans were already outside the town (e.g. in Penzberg), death sentences were still passed and executed. Today, with its wars in the Arab countries, in the Ukraine, with the Rohingyas and in the Congo, things have not gotten any better. It's all so horrible. It will never be fixed, and people have always turned to themselves for this reason, but only as sleepers, only superficially.

If you really come to this area of the Parco Nationale del Val Grande, you have to stay somewhere on Lake Maggiore. I can recommend the quite original, not overly frequented and also reasonably priced Albergo Park Paradiso in Ghiffa. Supposedly it was built as a spacious villa over a hundred years ago for a bishop and his mistress, beautiful garden, small pool, small rooms with balcony or terrace and above all run by a very modest elderly couple with their slightly disabled son. Perhaps in the meantime the old gentlemen no longer exist, who always prepared quite a good breakfast and dinner.

The contrast between the original owner and the present one could not be greater, which ideally promotes a meditation on cultural, spiritual, social, present and past perspectives. The garden of the hotel has been furnished with botanical features already by the bishop. It is also possible to walk directly from there upwards for half an hour in north-west direction and enjoy a great view from the Riserva Naturale Speciale (i.e. a small natural park) and its small sanctuary Chiesa del Sacro Monte della SS.

Trinità di Ghiffa, have. I am always amazed how people find in such small pilgrimage places idols, little pictures and other devotional objects with which they keep at bay the fear of the modern world, while the bishop not only made life easy for himself, but also made it pleasurable.

Or is it simply the longing for the early faith that the early Christians still possessed in the catacombs, taking on persecution and torture. Mostly it is the devotion to Mary, the Mother of God, to which the simple, afflicted by rural life and the old, left behind by life, cling without further perspective. Mostly it is the men who don't do sports, but watch the sports show every day, and thus let their lives melt away. Mostly it is those who have nothing, but who afford the main part of alcoholic drinks, and so do not get far. Smoking has been given up by many, as it is almost nowhere, but ill-temper, gluttony and other similar things are still preferred cultural goods, especially among the rich.

It must be appreciated that organizations such as Greenpeace, Human Right Watch, Amnesty- and Transparency-International care about the bad things in the world, but they themselves are already large enterprises, which one can join mostly only with donations. Direct collaboration, from which one can get confirmation, demands too much time. Years ago, I wanted to work as a doctor for the German Doctors, which at that time would have been called Doctors for the Third World, but I ran into difficulties. The founder's name was Bernhard Ehlen, he was a Jesuit, and he wanted me to live in very simple accommodations, since I was already paying for most of the work myself. I was refused a hotel of my own, probably because it did not fit the Jesuit's Christian ideal of poverty. It was certainly well-intentioned to let the First World doctors, like the employees of the Salvation Army, work at the level of the clients in the Third World. However, I felt too old for that, and I did not want to be controlled denominationally by the Jesuit. So I now supported a small infirmary in Kenya, which eased my conscience.

14. From Pokhara to Muktinath

At the end of the sixties of the last century the trekking
path from Pokhara to Muktinath in Nepal was opened.
That means that from then on treks to this area could be
made at all. I was lucky enough to go on this about seven
to eight days long trek (purely outward), shortly after it
was opened. It sounds surely old-fashioned and elitist
exaggerated, if now again the complaint comes that it
does not look like at that time there any more. But this
time it is really true. The Nepalese government had to
design a special program many years ago to remove the
trash and garbage of the trekking tourists. You meet
more tourists than locals on the trek today.

Short flight from Kathmandu to Pokhara, from there
probably exists a route directly through the valley of the
Kali Gandhaki river towards Muktinath. However, we, a
small group of four people and two porters, went straight
north via Ghandruk, Shikha, Tatopani, Ghasa, Jomosom
to Muktinath. There were no official accommodations
yet, but the local porters, a Tibetan and a Nepalese,
could always put us up in private houses where we could
sleep on the floor. We walked about eight hours every
day, often up and then down almost step-like paths, later
meeting the Kali Gandhaki valley in the upper part,
mostly along long and narrow slopes steadily upwards. I
remember well the tremendous moment when, walking
around a bend, we suddenly saw the almost eight thousand meter high Machapuchare in front of us.

Although the mountain giant was still some distance away, the sight was overwhelming and there was no doubt that the height dimensions here were different from those in the Alps. It is sometimes difficult to estimate the ratio of distance to height, but here it was clear and striking: one of those immense Himalayan giants, almost eight thousand meters high, from which one can tower over the world and thus be in possession of all abilities. These mountain monsters are memorials, castles of the gods, megalithic formations that have always been revered and feared, and rightly so. It was not possible for me to go on immediately. One had to remain sitting on a tree trunk and listen if one could not hear the rumbling or even a voice of the giant. It would certainly have brought one immediately to the center of the million-year-old primordial knowledge that this mountain has on its back.

Almost every day we ate only rice with lentil vegetables and sometimes something we brought with us, a can of peach compote or a few nuts. Already on the way we met people from Mustang, a small kingdom of its own of Tibetan origin, which lies high in the north on the border with Tibet. Access to Mustang was closed, which made this place particularly mysterious and interesting. Very Tibetan was also the costume and the heavy baskets carried by the men and women we met. But a permit to Mustang, which we had applied for before, could not be obtained. It was already difficult enough to get to Muktinath, which is quite a bit nearer. In the meantime, the Nepalese government has deposed the king of Mustang and taken over the territory of this very own people administratively. Since 2009 there is also a passable road and in the meantime tourist tours to Mustang are offered.

After all, Muktinath is a place of pilgrimage for Hindus and Buddhists alike. But like Jomosom, the last place before it, Muktinath wasn't at all good for lingering and introspection. I found it too dingy, too simple, too bare and too ugly. The place is located on one of the oldest hiking trails in Nepal, at an altitude of almost four thousand meters, and makes you feel the toughening up that used to be needed for the even further pilgrimage and trade route to Tibet. Somehow you get the feeling that you have to reach the final throne of the gods, the Potala in Lhasa. Roof of the world, heavenly castle and crowning dignity achieved exclusively through hardship and deprivation. But the distance to Muktinath was also enough.

We actually wanted to fly back to Pokhara from Jomosom, which had a miniature airfield, with a small plane. After days of waiting, an airplane finally arrived, but only officials got out of it, who controlled the airfield and finally closed it because of alleged deficiencies, so that we and several locals, who would not all have fit into the plane anyway, had to walk everything back again. We had already dismissed our porters, and so we had to look for the accommodations needed on the way and get the necessary food ourselves. But this proved to be difficult.

As strangers we were impure, religiously not clean enough, and so they let us sleep outside on the terrace at the most and also food was not so easy to get. Nevertheless, I would describe this trekking tour as the most impressive thing I have ever experienced in this regard. These tiny mountain villages, the gorges, the rhododendron bushes, the snow-covered giants, repeatedly a bath in the cold river. The path, surrounded on the left by Dhalaugiri and on the right by Annapurna, already gave tremendous impressions. They were a journey back in time to earlier centuries and thus to oneself. Undoubtedly there are many other possibilities to experience something like this today. I emphasize this again to escape the image of the eternally strict. Some things are still possible today, but then probably somewhere else.

However, if it has to be a tour of Mount Everest is questionable. As is well known, ascenders and descenders often meet there and this in addition in the particularly narrow places. Many deaths have already occurred and happen again every year. No one can accurately predict a change in the weather, and no one can really test their own strength beforehand. I have already tried to climb on the Ortler and on the big pinnacle in the Dolomites but it was too strenuous and too difficult, and so I have turned back already after an hour. Often I have not reached the summit of some beautiful mountain, because either the children were there and did not want to go further, and I had to turn back wistfully. But sometimes I also didn't manage the level of difficulty.

In life, if you achieve only half of the goals you set out to achieve, it's already great. The most important goal is - I have already hinted at it several times - to really and in the full sense become a human being (tripartite one) and then to include transcendence in exactly this already mapped out path. Because only in this way it is guaranteed that my expression 'really man in the full sense' is not a mythical squiggle and vice versa this great truth of what I have just called transcendence is included in the expression. I could choose here again from the field of psychoanalysis the term of the good 'inner object-constancy'. However, it is very academic and probably means a positive, mature, successful, inner firmness.

When Goethe says in Faust: 'For precisely when concepts are lacking, then a word presents itself at the right time,' I would turn this quotation around and say: 'For whenever one can no longer manage with so many words, then a definite concept is salutary. So perhaps the term charisma still proves to be most appropriate for the state of the soul in catharsis and especially in the surrender of these pass-words. Everyone is a charismatic when he finds himself in his inward looking and his 'full speaking'. The 'full speaking' is also a revealing speaking and not only a simple communicating. In the charisma the subject-related signs reveal themselves, so to speak the innermost of each one.

Because the usual sign is only something for someone, but the sign of a subject is a signifier, the already mentioned node of meaning, which can be fuzzy, imprecise and indeterminate, but which counts! Therefore all information, communication and digitalization is of no use, if it serves only the mediation of usual signs. What is important is not that a human subject exchanges with another subject, but that they reveal themselves to each other, admit something to each other, open themselves in mutual curiosity and respect. Curiosity understood as emotional interest and respect as special appreciation of the other. Together they have a constructive effect, and that is what counts.

We were able to talk with the people from Mustang only for some time, mediated by our interpreting carriers. We expressed our curiosity and our respect for their original way of life and physical fitness. And they also appreciated us by expressing the wish that we should visit them in their country. But that was not possible, and so we said goodbye with the greatest possible linguistic, mimic and gestural regret. How could we integrate their proud simplicity into our lives? What could we bring or do for them, if we would really get there one day?

It behaves like with the life of the early men, whom we cannot meet any more, but we need only - as I have described it already further above - to put ourselves into them, to study them and to love them. Then we can feel their bronzed, tanned and furrowed faces, which, as in the case of the people of Mustang, in spite of all their austerity, seemed taut, clear and somehow pure, i.e. not like ours, which are puffed up, used up, worn out and distorted. They have become so uninteresting from the hustle and bustle with which we will soon be rushing from wellness event to wellness event that one no longer delves into them. So from the early humans one can learn just as well the completely relaxed informality, as from the people in the Himalaya.

Because you don't always have to look for a quiet corner or a secluded roof terrace to have that ' feeling of inner fitness' that the people from Mustang conveyed. They are fit not only because of the loads they carry for kilometers over the mountain passes, but because they are so unified and so strong inside. All the hauling is rather disadvantageous, because with this work they do not grow old. Most of the time they use their yaks as beasts of burden just like in Bhutan or other Himalayan countries. The animals are tough, adapted to extreme altitudes and so strong that their blood is used against diseases (the animals are not killed but only bled, but you have to drink the blood, for which there is a special festival in Mustang).

We preferred to drink the water from the bubbling mountain streams that feed the Kali Gandhaki. You don't have to drink blood and whether you should mix it into the normal bourgeois food, I also think is questionable. The gourmet chef H. This-Benckhard describes with relish how to bind the sauce for roast rabbit not with flour or egg, but with blood.[59] Shortly before serving, the fresh blood must be stirred into the gravy. The author does not reveal where to keep the fresh blood, but this is not about whether it is better to be a vegetarian or a cannibal. Rather, one can see well from these examples what signifiers are and why they are the ones that count. For one senses very quickly in this talk of oral pleasure and palate tickling and of the power that one can directly ingest that the signifier "blood" glows devilishly red in it. This-Benckhard's spicy gourmet stories can easily tip over into the macabre of a totemic blood meal.

That it is so difficult, after all, to transfer the unbiased happiness of the primary peoples to us, when we give them a little modern know how in return. There is no such thing as the primal blissful manager, the paradisiacal sex freak, the happy bureaucrat. There are numerous intermediate stages on the way from the happily biased to the neurosis-ridden success man, but they are all no better. Would a house on the slopes of the Himalayas, with a grandiose view into the distance, help? A small Kenyan villa on the beach of Msambweni? Or a roof terrace apartment in Central Park in New York? No. It's more likely to be found where Tschuang Tse writes: in the "realm of silence.

"Realm of silence. I was in it that time.

---

[59] This-Benckhard, H., Kulinarische Geheimnisse (culinary secrets), Piper (2001) S. 229

Really . . .

Heightened, new, complete.

Silence of the essential.

Return to the ground.

The useless finally expelled . . ."

"Horses and buffaloes have four legs - that's what I call heaven. . . Take care that the human does not destroy the heavenly (in you); take care that the intentional (gu) does not destroy the necessary (ming) (in you)."

But you probably need both. They only have to be in good relation to each other. I remind again of the concept of hyperspace, whose lines follow Einstein's topology and which also has something to do with the visual, the identical or naively analogous. For in hyperspace one does not refer to the geometral or vanishing point of classical perspective, which ends at the horizon line, but to a center that flows into the 'baseline', subject line, which can represent a vision or a wall. Withdrawn into the concave mirror of the cerebrum further back than is usual for perception and identification. So can the 'return into the ground' be clearly located nowadays. As one will be able to understand the universe only from this point of highest concentrations of dark matter/energy, so also oneself only by the return to the 'ground line' of the imaginary order where the 'useless is driven out'.

15. Amalfi Coast

With a small car from the airport in Naples, you are quickly so far up on Vesuvius that you only have a good half hour walk ahead of you. The view into the crater is tremendous and one remembers the pictures of Pompei after the volcanic eruption in 79: all the figures buried in the ash rain, the futile escape of some down to the harbor to still take a ship out to sea, where they were caught up by the ash rain just the same. However, if you want to do a real hike, it is better to go to Positano and from there walk the 'Sentiero degli Dei' to Praiano (before Amalfi). You can take the bus to Montepertuso or even to Nocelle, then you save the bit on the pass road and it's only three hours of walking.

High above the Amalfi Coast, there are always wonderful views down to the sea and the coastal towns and far over to Capri, where the Swedish doctor A. Munthe lived his famous life for more than seventy years. He could still feel like the master of a small paradise, having previously worked as a doctor in several large European cities. At times he ran a practice for the lowest strata of the population, then again only for high society. He was also the personal physician of the Swedish King Victoria. His Villa San Michele in Anacapri was visited by many famous personalities, and from the magnificent garden one still has a magnificent view of the sea. In his autobiography, however, he mixed fact with transfigured fantasies, which amounts to narcissistic self-sublimation. He was able to live his own dream and even describe it, probably because many women raved about him and because the legendary idealistic was still considered desirable. A subtle closeness to the world is more appealing to us today, an example of how we can do things better today if we have learned from the past.

Also the trail 'Sentiero degli Dei' is characterized by constant ups and downs, while passing through three or four deep slopes. Several times small holm oak groves, columnar cypresses, mulberry trees and magnolias in bloom. Along the path there are poppies, sage, broom and purslane. One hardly encounters a single person. Finally down to Praiano, from where you take the bus back to Positano, not without having visited the church in Vettica Maggiore. The way from Amalfi over hundreds (or is it thousands) of stairs up directly to Ravello, the most beautiful place of the whole area, is also very exhausting. A slightly longer way is via Scala and is not as arduous. The park and panoramic terrace of Villa Cimbrone in Ravello are the highlight here apart from the park of Villa Rufolo, which is said to have inspired

Richard Wagner to write Klingsor's Magic Garden. This brings me back to a topic that can be rehashed a bit.

I don't understand much of Wagner's music, whereby I ask myself once again whether one really has to 'understand' music fully and what that means. The music philosopher T. W. Adorno, in his 'Dialectic of Enlightenment', argues that the true musician not only absorbs a concerto in every nuance and respect, but also fully understands and grasps it, from the past related to this music, through the present, into the future. Four or five further gradations follow with regard to this understanding of music, whereby I would have to confess to the approximately second level of the music listener, namely to the one in which one hears a few melodies quite gladly but in the moment where one notices that it is now about the implementation, then the recapitulation or about the tonic, dominant etc., the desire loses a little.

As a student, Wagnerian mythology enthralled me for a while, and I have now heard four or five of his operas. And in the Villa Rufolo in Ravello one could participate in a piano recital, which was quite nice - something like included in the hotel package and the guided tour through the garden. One is then taken care of all around. Compensating was the place on the terrace of the hotel Villa Maria in the evening with view far down to the sea and the flashing lights. And with the caresses of the wind passing through the great Mediterranean pine to soothe the heat and put one in a contemplative mood. Promptly I had another such experience of 'hearing' from the unconscious. A 'hearing' that is so near and yet so far, for it concerns one and is thus more than hearing good advice. "It's ash-crumbly" was the 'ultra-reduced', the pass-word, this time, which didn't sound so nice and rosy, but rather a bit gloomy.

But it was true. I felt this way not only because I had already written sixteen books about my meditation method, and the response was sparse, really frustrating, in short: 'ash-crumbly'. But also in the depth of my soul there was still something 'ash-crumbly'. The sexual-aggressive primal scene I mentioned was haunting me for many years, the aggressive of the father was mixed in the unconscious fantasy and dreams (an expression constantly discussed in psychoanalysis) with the sexual of the mother and connected with me as the sometimes more sadistic, sometimes more masochistic object. It took me some time to turn it off, because it kept coming back. Only with the help of such and similar pass-words it disappeared completely.

The whole world will turn to ashes one day, and now I can write about it, because the method of treating the unconscious imagination so directly can also help others. It is a huge difference whether another person, whom you may appreciate, says this to you, whether you give in to it yourself, or whether it shakes you up from the inside with such a saying. The philosopher of religion E. Troeltsch emphasized this 'being touched' from within as a category of cognition. Nothing is solid, 'It wobbles', he often said to counter the rigid writings of the straight-forward, ultra-orthodox philosophers and cardinals who only have their career and power status in mind. 'Id wobbles' and 'Id's ash-crumbly'. Freud could only grasp this 'Id' as the 'reservoir of drives', Lacan called 'Id' 'the subject of the unconscious'. We are far too much 'I' and not 'Id', the real subject, but at the same time the helper coming from the Other in ourselves.

And how should one be 'Id' and at the same time helper? One cannot only follow subjective impulses. One also needs a 'baseline', a procedure, a 'science of the subject', a subject-related method that gives one the security to deal with oneself well and correctly. Not all pass-words are accurate, helpful and interpretable. Some are critical, negative, admonishing and condemning. But this also happens in a good psychoanalysis. Freud even said that the analytic treatment only progresses when 'negative transferences' also take place, i.e. one has a rage against the therapist and finds him idiotic. Often patients break off the therapy in the 'negative transference', in meditation this cannot happen. One is too aware that in the end it is one's own thoughts that get to one. But this can and must be endured.

I have written that with Staemmler's 'dialogical self' one does not get far in psycho-physical development. Staemmler himself had - as mentioned - a problem with Freud, although he based himself on his teaching. His teacher F. Perls himself also struggled with this teacher/disciple, father/son problem and sought out Freud to discuss it. But the dialogue there lasted only five minutes and contented itself with polite phrases. Perls had to recognize that he felt great sorrow at not having been able to 'talk man to man' with Freud. But this is exactly not what he could have learned from Freud. He was missing that even as a more mature man he had not been able to talk to the father (to the father of psychoanalysis), and so in later life he rejected psychoanalysis as did his student Staemmler.

Exactly this mixture of real and metaphorical father does not come into play in the 'dialogical self'. From this, perhaps, Wittgenstein's 'trialogic' is even better understood. This triad of speaking prompted Lacan to call one of his seminars 'Les noms du père'. Les noms du père (The names of the father), Les non du père (The no of the father) and Les non Dupes errent (The non-stupid err), represents a formulaic triple formulation, a formal 'trialogy' in that through a homophony (word sound overlap) in French all three statements sound the same, although they contain three completely different and, moreover, very original utterances. The structure of this sentence is thus like that of the exercise formulas (formula-words) chosen by me ambiguous, one can commit oneself to no meaning alone. But this is exactly how the unconscious works, this is also how the Other works. One has to go through something like this in order to come to a real and true statement of the unconscious. This is not achieved by the 'dialogical self'.

The small alleys of Amalfi should be seen and also the 1200 year old cathedral with crypt and cloister as well as the busy square from which about fifty wide steps lead up to the cathedral. All a bit picturesque, but also aesthetically and devotionally strong, because the bones of St. Andrew the Apostle are said to have been there for almost a thousand years. They were brought to safety in 1203 before the Turks would have captured them in Constantinople. This hanging on a few bones of the apostle, on Buddha's tooth or a whisker of Mohammed is already a world of its own, which has something rotten-morbid about it. I dreamed once in the cellar of my house to see a bishop with the miter standing at an altar, everything dipped in gold shine. Astonished but also suspecting that something could not be right, I carefully felt for the figure. At that moment, everything crumbled into a musty, sticky dust that took one's breath away. The unconscious demonstrator had shown reality and told the truth.

16. The Euganean Hills

These hills in Veneto are actually more for bicycle tours.
The trails are not far, though not without ups and downs.
It's best to ride from one of the beautiful villas to another, as these are the highlights. Now and then there is also
a nice view from one of the hills. You might stay in
Monte Grotto or in Galziniano. Less recommendable is
Abano Therme, which has always been a retirement
home and certainly still is. The bicycle tour starts at Villa Emo capodilista in the northeast of the hill range. A
splendid building, which can be rented - probably at
horrendous prices. Interior decoration and frescoes are
definitely worth seeing.

Afterwards you can drive over one of the hills to the
Abbazia di Praglia, a large Benedictine monastery with a
magnificent chapter house and church. Here again frescoes (e.g. wall fresco Deposition of the Cross by Titian's
pupil Girolamo Tessari), paintings and several cloisters.
The route finally continues to Villa dei Vescovi, a 16th
century Venetian villa in Torreglia. The villa is a large,
square, simple example of Renaissance architecture in
Venetia. It contains important frescoes and furnishings
to match, and also offers a sweeping view of the countryside.

Continuing on, in about half an hour, you will reach
Villa Barbarigo, where the 17th century baroque garden
is the most special and fantastic thing about it. It is arranged in such a way that there are intersections and

lines of sight to the different areas, such as the boxwood labyrinth, the magnificent 'Bagno di Diana' (Diana's bath), the rabbit island, the large fish ponds, three small lakes, 16 fountains and various statues. Under an ancient coniferous tree in the middle it is good to rest, remembering Stefan George's poem:

"Come to the dead-said park and look:
The gleam of distant smiling shores . . .
There take the deep-full yellow - the soft gray-smook . ."

From Villa Barbarigo it would then not be far to Arquà Petrarca, a small stately nest at medium altitude with a beautiful marketplace, church and pomegranate trees. But this highlight is better saved for the next day. It is not only the small town, but the villa of the poet Petrarch (1304 - 1374) and of course the poet himself, for which - all in all - you have to take some time. The beautiful 'Casa Petrarca' is surrounded by a small garden, where the poet had grown wine, apples and spices. Today box trees, oleanders, pines, laurels, olives and cherry trees grow there. The condition in which the visitor finds

Petrarca's retirement home today dates back to a 16th century successor owner. He had the upper floor painted with splendid and interesting frescoes that refer to the main works of the poet.

Crucial for Petrarch and us as his tourists investigating him was the poet's encounter with 'Laura'. It may have been Laura de Noves, a married woman from Avignon, belonging to better circles. The story is strongly reminiscent of that of Dante and Beatrice, because Petrarch never exchanged a word with Laura and probably saw her only once very briefly. It was probably this that made 'Laura' a goddess and an unattainable lover. In his 'Canzoniere', a cycle of 366 poems and sonnets, the poet sings of his erotomanic image in skillful lyricism. However, one must not believe that the poet suffered from this seemingly unhappy love. He needed her - remaining prudish towards her - only for his art.

For he played a phonological game with Laura's name and wrote a lyric poetry that ingeniously deals with words like laureato (honored), l'aurora (dawn), lauro (laurel), aureo (golden), aura (breeze, aura) and Cupid's 'aurato strale' (the golden arrow) etc.. All poetisms that should point not only to the beloved, but - as literary connoisseurs say - also to him, the poet himself. Petrarch was a bit vain. The woman was therefore probably a means to an end, was predominantly the poet's muse. Laura was the virtual and symbolic erotic, the happy paper on which he wrote, the laurel wreath he could finally place on his own head. For in 1341 Petrarch was crowned poet (poeta laureatus) at the Capitol in Rome, and relations with the jury are said to have played a role. He was a bohemian and at the same time a patrician, one who knew how to live. After all, he lived to be seventy years old, which was already a lot at that time.

To make a woman, who exists almost only poetically, into a heroin and goddess worshipped in unhappy love, has always been a clever trick in literature. Goethe, too, has his Werther fall into schizoid-histrionic states toward his beloved, which eventually drive him to suicide and enabled his author to achieve his literary breakthrough. Goethe acknowledged with a shrug of his shoulders that many imitators of Werther also committed suicide. If it didn't work out with the real lover - Lady von Stein - he had to find another, invented figure of light, who could break the lover of Goethe, but with whom he could also succeed.

Also for S. Freud women (the hysterics) had been to a considerable extent means to the end of the invention of his psychoanalysis. It was he who had first put women on the couch and then positioned himself close to them, only to find out - trickily enough - who they were. But none of this can diminish the achievements of Petrarch or Freud and all the other cultural heroes in whom woman must be written as 'T h e', that is, with the definite and universalizing article. Lacan, in fact, thinks that 'T h e woman' does not exist at all, that this or that exists, but whoever thinks that he has found 'T h e woman', the absolute woman per se, is probably crazy. But poets and scientists are allowed to use a certain madness that is close to genius.

However, what gives further importance to the visit to Arquà Petrarca for my article in this mountain climbing book is the fact that Petrarca was the first 'tourist' mountain climber. In any case, even today he is praised in this sense by alpine associations. In 1336, he climbed Mont Ventoux in Provence and has since been considered the 'father of mountaineering'. In addition, he had a certain awe-inspiring experience on the summit, when he read there a word from Augustine's Confessiones that had been opened by chance.[60] Having become famous, he was later appointed to the court of the Cardinal of Avignon, after which he was also envoy to Milan for eight years. Besides his cycle of poems, his 'Dialogue' written in Latin and some madrigals are also peculiarities of his work.

But now we move on to Monselice, a slightly larger town on the southern edge of the Euganean Hills. The first documented mention of Monselice dates back to 568 and refers to the capture of the town by the Lombards. On the small ridge in the town is Villa Duodo, to which one can make a pilgrimage up for another beauti-

---

[60] By the way, Augustine acted in the same way. He opened the Bible at a randomly chosen place when he thought he heard a voice in the neighboring garden saying: 'Look and read'. Of course, it was then exactly the passage that - as he himself thought - fitted him and made him a preacher of faith.

ful panoramic view. On certain days there is a nice market in the main square where everything is traded.

The Euganean Hills have become important mainly for the spas with mud treatments and their medicinal waters. But neither fango nor warm water can do great things. For the prevention of arthrosis, the best thing is a lot of exercise without stressing the joints, i.e. swimming, cycling and gymnastics on the mat, as well as losing weight. Mountain hiking - I mentioned it before - doesn't do so well here. Artificial joint replacement has become routine today, but the surgical risk remains. At least the warm water has a relaxing effect and promotes contemplation. And so, in the end, we cycle on to Ferrara, an ancient city with a magnificent cathedral and numerous palazzi. Moreover, Ferrara is the city of cyclists, so you are in the right company. A few churches and a leaning tower are the landmarks.

This time I write nothing to my self-therapeutic procedure, because it could become now slowly too monotonous. I merely add a few remarks in the sense of Petrarch, whose musical play with vowel or syllable repetitions I have quoted. The literary scholar S. Bayerl, in her study "From the language of music to the music of language", has presented a comprehensive account of this subject, which revolves around the models of language oriented to the 'spirit of music'.[61] Rhythm and verse,

---

[61] Bayerl, S., Von der Sprache der Musik zur Musik der Sprache, Königshausen & Neumann (2002)

often have a metric that served not only better declamation, but also better mnemonics. In this sense, Bayerl refers to "language composers" and "dialectists" such as E. Jandl, who "splits words", who speaks of the "snile (instead of smile) of MonaLisa", and of many other word games, which I cannot reproduce here in the English translation from the German. The reader will notice, however, that it is nevertheless again about the B(r)uchstaben (broken letters), which are so dear to me.

17. La Palma, Gran Canaria and Lanzarote

The green island La Palma offers many and beautiful hiking trails. Some recommend as an introduction to the hiking tours in the center of the island to make the Cumbrecita round around the large volcanic cauldron, the Caldera de Taburiente. The path is easy and can be done in only one hour. More challenging is to try a first trip all the way south to the Volcanes de Teneguía. You first go to the crater rim of San Antonio, then to the Teneguía crater, which erupted or reformed in 1971. The trail is similar to the northeast trail in Madeira, lots of rock, lava, sand and the thick-leafed plants of the genus Aeonium. The forty or so known species of Aeonium are found only in the Canary Islands, especially in La Palma. Something special are also the many dragon trees on the island, which exist in this quantity only there.

A hike through the laurel forest in the northeast is also interesting. Many take the route through the narrow and low tunnels from Casa del Monte, but the other way around, from the end of the highway, you don't have to struggle as much and hike through the wonderful Barrancos del Agua and back again. In total, there are over thirty route descriptions in the hiking guides, which I don't have to go into in detail here. In any case, the island is not overcrowded and large hotel blocks still do not exist (2011). However, more recent information (2021) speaks a completely different language, namely that of 'ever faster', 'ever higher', 'ever richer', 'ever dumber'.

This is quite in contrast to Gran Canaria, where hotel and apartment blocks line up in the east and south. Nevertheless, in the northwest of Gran Canaria there are fantastic vertical cliffs and the interior is still worth exploring. Admittedly, hardly anyone will still succeed in finding the 'blue flower' of romance up in the central mountains, as the famous Spanish poet Unamuno once managed to do. Unfortunately, I could no longer find out the name of the flowering plant, which was probably extremely rare and was discovered by Unamuno there in the complete solitude of the rough rocks. In any case, the poet describes this unexpected discovery as a meditative experience, which it undoubtedly was and which he also needed. For his life was completely torn between art, philology, politics of the most diverse directions, complicated private life, philosophy, the learning of numerous languages, poetry, finally the banishment and a rather unspecific end.

In his philosophical book 'The Tragic Sense of Life', Unamuno wrote: 'Everything vital is anti-rational, and everything rational is anti-vital', a seemingly irresolvable contradiction. In the life of every human being there is ultimately found this limit of the insoluble, of the impossible, as it also concernedß the Lacanien 'Real'. The Real does not so much concern external reality, but an internal boundary that one is always bumping up against. It is reminiscent of Marlene Haushofer's novel 'The Wall', which is invisible and yet impenetrable. The philosopher Clement Rosset, whom I have already quoted as saying that the real becomes particularly effective when one is in harmony with one's doubles, i.e. with oneself and the Other (capital A), sees it similarly.[62]

This has namely something true-delusional in itself, because if the human being insists on being perceived by the Other absolutely, the real can show itself everywhere. If one exists only and exclusively when the big 'you' (a personalized real) perceives one, one has no I anymore. The real is an eternal, but also blooming shadow. "In a psychoanalysis, for example, the secret that the analysand most jealously guards, namely that he actually has nothing to hide, would have to be revealed, and this can only be done with a certain violence similar to that of rape in the confessional box," Rosset writes.[63]

M. Haushofer's protagonist in the cited novel is also in harmony only in a pathological way with her doubles,

---

[62] Rosset, C., Das Reale, Traktat über die Idiotie (The Real, Treatise on Idiocy), Suhrkamp (1988) pp. 50-63.
[63] Rosset, C., Das Reale in seiner Einzigartigkeit (The Real in its Uniqueness), Merve (2000) pp. 154-168.

the men reduced to the purely masculine. When one of them suddenly breaks through the wall and kills two of her animals with an axe, she shoots him. The real, then, cannot be so easily mastered, nor measured, nor properly defined, since no example or intrinsic value can be assigned to it. It remains unique and thus refuses any interpretation or characterization. "For example, the objects of laughter, horror, desire, film, and music give rise to alienating and exemplary perceptions of the real. This deception is, in fact, the mirror of man trapped by the expectation of an event that did not take place where it should," writes Rosset again.

And further: "Since we can thus probably never get used to the real, we try to change it ourselves by working on it, correcting it and expanding it and striving to smooth its raw appearance mirror-like. In doing so, it is a matter of literally keeping reality away from oneself and protecting oneself from the intrusion of the real by means of loopholes and castles in the air. . . Basically, man must reject the real, since it leads him into the conflict between recognition of reality or preservation of the self. The only way to accept it seems to be only that of complete stupidity, of pure thoughtlessness, or that of self-annihilation. Thus, in order to survive, the subject must decide for itself and thus against the real."

Here the philosopher exaggerates, because a retreat to the most elementary of oneself is, in order to be able to proceed from there - at least 'ultra-reduced' in Rays an Speaks and thus nevertheless positively - is possible. I comment later again on this conundrum of the real, which is therefore somehow - constantly incomprehensible - there. It is a body without form like the lava landscape on Lanzerote, which I still want to mention briefly. The Timanfaya National Park in the southwest of the island is the most interesting area and extends over 51.07 square kilometers. 32 volcanic cones were formed here at that time, the last eruption occurred in 1824. Buses that take you through the volcanic landscape start at Islote de Hilario. This tour is recommended, because you get close to the lava. You can not walk alone through the park. There are hot lava spots everywhere, where you can see the glow under the stones.

At Islote de Hilario, a park employee demonstrates how much it is still bubbling under the earth's surface. He puts some brushwood into a hole in the ground. After a few seconds it burns brightly. Red-grey, orange and black rock-lava-rock masses create a scenario, which from its physical side actually reminds of something like the real, even if it is only its end product and thus represents more the outer reality. Lanzerote offers other reasons to visit, namely the impact that the architect and culturalist Cesar Manrique left here. He recognized early on the danger of mass tourism and the associated monstrous hotel castles and turned to ecological-purist architecture.

So he created only a few idiosyncratic buildings, but in the long run this 'Small is beautiful', which also elsewhere the eco-psychologists have written on their flags, can not be held on Lanzerote. As I could read, there are at present already more than twenty five-star hotel palaces on the island matching the more than twenty years that Cesar Manriques is already dead. However, the 'Small is beautiful' reminds me of a completely different phenomenon, namely the method of AMSR (Autonomous Sensory Meridian Response), in which people bring themselves into euphoric-cathartic states even with very small and insignificant sounds. I have already mentioned the electric toothbrush, which, placed close by, calms down the toddler quite quickly when he is whining and restless. AMSR adepts even download their own videos created for this purpose, which show and let listen to light scratching, rubbing or grinding noises on various occasions, in order to achieve the same relaxation and chill-out feeling.

But the whole thing is a joke and a noise fetishism at the same time. Every modern person knows by now that lying in a foreign city on the fifth floor of a hotel with the window open, you can use the soundscape far below just as much for catharsis. The quiet and monotonous traffic noise, the distant chatter of human sounds and the whispering of the city and the wind provide the ideal auditory backdrop for calming and rapture. One resorts to an atavism, to an element of reciprocity essential in early childhood (sounds in the womb?) or early humanity (primary speech sounds). It is as if one has a conversation with the 'universal murmur' of the unconscious, which this time comes from within as well as from without.

However, the AMSR subjects are constantly on the lookout for ever different, partly quite bizarre stimuli, which actually distracts them from the essential part of the mumbling, namely that which comes suggesting the truth from within, and leads them further and further away. Thus they will never get to the so important passwords from the unconscious, but remain in the hum of an infantile catharsis. For intimate bodily sounds are very popular and lead into a delirium of early fusion experiences, which were necessary, for example, for early humans to communicate, since they had few of the modern speech sounds. Catharsis is important in meditation, but it must come from inner experience (inner touch) while accompanying the dialogic-trialogic.

The same that is true of sound fetishism is also true of fetishism practiced with the image, the pictorial imagination, the iconic, or the pixel. Whereas 150 years ago we were only exposed to the images of nature and the paintings of individual painters, today we are concerned with the confrontation, a billion times more frequent, of that which is directly visualized through photographs, television, film, computers, illustrated magazines, YouTube, Instagram, etc. We have almost inevitably become icon and pixel fetishists, and therefore no longer know which images are actually authoritative for us and which are not. I have already mentioned this fact in the case of idyllophilia and visual art, and I must emphasize it again here. In the past, we only relied on visions of Christ, iconoclasts were en vogue. Today we only have to choose a little bit if we really want to see everything that is presented to us. We would already get into ecstasy by the less-is-more.

What that means, everyone must decide for himself. That just the somewhat barren, not too colorful landscapes are the most beautiful, is probably more or less true. Painting or photographing oneself has always been a way out of the flood misery caused by the pixel world or stultifying TV productions. But for the time being again back to La Palma. In the meantime (2016) there are obviously nevertheless two large hotels in the west of the island, which has also always the better weather. The Roque de los Muchachos, a volcanic cone over 2400 meters high catches the clouds and leaves them over the eastern side. But at the moment I am writing this translation into English, the volcano Cumbra Vieja has been raging for many weeks in the southern part of the island.

Located more in the center of the island, a long tunnel connects the east and west sides, so you can quickly traverse the width of the island. You can quickly look over to the west every day, if you live in the east - as I did at that time - where the vegetation is even more lush. It is even better to cross to El Hierro, which has been declared a protected area by Unesco and is a scenic paradise. And of course I have to point out the whistling language still practiced there, which explains so well that not only music and language go into each other, but also already the intimate tone from the sphere of the other almost reaches to the trialogue.

18. The Gorges of Verdon

Coming from the French Nice, via Cannes and Grasse, the world capital of perfume, one can easily reach the town of Castellane in Haute-Provence in a day. A seemingly unspecial town and yet, the small restaurant north of the main square and the equally nice hotel not far from it make it exclusive and cozy. Often the remote, unobtrusive simple places in the south of France are the best alternative to mass tourism. Well, but if you then hiked through the Verdon Gorge and continue on to St. Tropez, you're stuck again traveling exactly where everyone is going. The only way out is then to stay there, in St. Tropez, in the small, angular hotel Maison Blanche.

But first a look at the daring gorge, for example, during a hike from the Col d'Olivier and along the Cascades de Saint-Maurin at the end of the Gorges du Verdon, until they flow into the waters of the lake Lac de Sainte-Croix. The lower waterfall gives a fantastic touch. You can see the so-called travertine folds in the limestone, formed by the calcareous water. They can store CO_2, but release it when heated. The walk goes once along the top and once along the bottom of the gorge. Everything is impressive, and so I am back to thinking about the real and its relation to reality. For what distinguishes the two, if one starts from the iconology just discussed?

For I. Kant, God was not so important, because there was (as already indicated), after all, the 'thing-in-itself', which was also nothing else than the 'real' I just mentioned and Rosset highlighted. The 'thing in itself' was that which could not be grasped like the usual things of everyday reality. Schopenhauer therefore meant that this 'thing in itself' was nothing other than the will, a willing that he contrasted with the imagination (the objects). Freud finally turned it into the unconscious desire, the drive, which is also opposed to the objects. And Lacan went one step further, saying that desire is not only unconscious to the subject itself, but is also foreign, other, to it, L'Autre (the Other). He said that the unconscious is constructed like the language of the Other, like an ça parle, an 'Id Speaks'. 'Id Speaks' in a language without words. To understand this 'Id Speaks' from the unconscious as something transcendent, thus closes the circle back to Kant and to God.

From the story of Samuel in the Old Testament to Spinoza, this cycle from A to Z and back to A is well known. Samuel's mother got a child only after desperate efforts, prayers and visits to the temple priest Eli. In fact, her husband's other wife had already given birth to several children, and when she finally had her Samuel, she said something like that he was actually the child of God, and one day gave him to the chief priest Eli in the temple. There he served for many years, and one night he dreamed that Eli, the ancient ruler of the temple, had called him to him. Did he perhaps want to give him his blessing, his last word? No, the old man only said, "Lie down again, I did not call you, you were dreaming."

But soon after, Samuel heard his name again, rushed back to Eli, who again gave him a comforting farewell with the same words. So it took - as it often is in legends of saints - a third time. Again Samuel heard very clearly and no longer in a dream - perhaps shortly afterwards or in a meditative state - his name called. Again he went to Eli, who again sent him away, but this time had noticed that there was something special about his foster son Samuel. Therefore he said to Samuel, "When you hear the call again, say at once, "Speak, your servant hears!" And so Samuel finally heard the voice of his God as Eli had suggested to him and felt called to higher things.[64]

Today we would say that it was the core unconscious that had called Samuel, the image- and word-real (imaginary and verbal signifier, that Rays and Speaks in particularly close, successful, mature combination). For this unconscious consists in part of the repressed, of Samuel's mother and father problems. It sounds particularly impressive that the mother gives away the son she wants so

---

[64] 1. Samuel 1,1 – 3,15

much, as if her only intention was to show her rival that she has also given birth to a son and successor in the family, and does not actually need him for herself. Or that she was so ultraorthodox that she did it only for her own salvation, for her own glory. Such a trauma, namely being given away and not wanted for its own sake, might have triggered in him the waking sound, the call for himself to be confirmed and recognized in his identity. This desire for recognition crosses in him with the recognition of an unconscious desire, perhaps that of being loved by the father?

Thus Samuel's wake-up call conveys exactly that voice with which one can hear the pass-words. It is quite characteristic, namely in such a way that one really believes at the beginning that it is a foreign voice. But still in the thawing out from the unconscious, at least still in the last moment, the voice becomes recognizable as that of the own thoughts. So the crux lies in the pass word, which indeed sometimes comes across as if spoken with the voice of a stranger (as if from the depths or far away, as if strange and yet peculiar). And it does not reflect the opinion of any particular someone, but just that of the great I-Other in everyone himself.

So, as much as the story of Samuel correlates with the essence of the Speaks, the verbal signifier, the story of Daniel, as the dream interpreter in the Old Testament, correlates with the essence of the Id Rays, the imaginary signifier.[65] The king Nebuchadnezer began to have dis-

---

[65] Daniel 2, 1-48

turbing dreams and sent for his scholars and magicians. But the king persisted in not wanting to tell the contents of the dream, to which they responded just as persistently, insisting that without a knowledge of what the king had dreamed, they could not help him. Now Nebuchadnezzar wanted to kill all the scholars, although at that time they did it in the same way as the psychoanalysts would do it today; however, today no patient would think of asking for a dream interpretation without telling the dream, and the therapists are also not as smart as Daniel was.

When Daniel heard about Nebuchadnezzar's plan, he immersed himself in the image of his god, and thus got to know approximately what the king had dreamed. Just like a therapist convinced of the imaginary, of the Rays in the unconscious (what the modern psychoanalysts, however, do not know and use), it was clear to him that a king had most probably dreamed of power and the question of maintaining his power by suitable successors. And so he told Nebuchadnezer that the latter had probably seen a tall figure in the dream, the head made of gold and other metallic layers underneath. The gold, he said, was the king himself, then came others less successful ones, but at last all would merge into one infinite kingdom. This calmed Nebuchadnezer beyond measure and he made Daniel the chief prefect over large parts of Babylon. Can Daniel be made a role model for psychoanalysts?

Yes, but they would have to offer their patients to practice Analytic Psychocatharsis at home independently of the therapy sessions. Then the emphatically pictorial would come more into play and could enrich the literal interpretations. And so once again briefly to St. Tropez. Opposite the aforementioned Hotel Maison Blanche is a beautiful elongated square, partly overshadowed by trees, partly populated with market stalls and restaurants, where wonderful marinated or gratinated artichoke dishes are served outdoors. Then, via Rue François Sibilli, you can quickly get to the harbor to look at the yachts of the oligarchs, where you have to wonder if it's really still a pleasure to see one yacht right next to another, hundreds of them, like herrings in a can. Of course, we are all God, each in his own way, but you can't show it to everyone in the right way.

19. Sheep Mountain, Austria

The Sheep Mountain (Schafkopf) borders south of the Moon-Lake (Mondsee) in the Salzkammergut, where I grew up as a child. From our house in the village of Mondsee, we could see him every day, his sheep's head and back in a lying position. As little children, we kept thinking that one day he might rise up as a sheep and run away. But he never ran away and we never got there, not even to the southeast tip of the lake. Even during the war and shortly after, no one considered making an excursion or a hike to the surrounding area, certainly not further away or up a mountain. Thus, the Schafkopf, as a powerful guardian of the lake, remained a great mystery for us for a long time.

It was only much later with my own children that I managed to climb it. One went up quite far from St. Wolfgang with the rack railroad and then continued on foot. I have already spoken of the inhibiting effect of children in mountaineering, and so it was here. I could not climb the so long desired summit, the children grumbled and whined already after a few hundred meters and so I had to turn back shortly before the summit of the Schafkopf without having achieved anything. Truly no reflection and relaxation experience. After all, the view down to the lake and into the wide surroundings is very impressive. Lake Atter (Attersee) and Lake Wolfgang (Wolfgangsee) can also be glimpsed.

But much more interesting for us kids was the Dragon Wall (Drachenwand), which is located more to the side-south of the lake. This rock face has a hole several meters wide at the top (small picture on the right). According to the stories, which we heard again and again from all sides and which increased the authenticity strongly, the devil should have broken in the wild-racing flight by the rock wall and have hurled the fragment furiously into the lake, where one could see a small point of it still protruding from the water. With such slight shocks, accordingly, the soul life began with me. There was the majestic Sheep Mountain and the eerie Dragon Wall next to each other. Beautiful, strong, shuddering, beguiling, wild, astonishing-frightening and jubilatory experiences are a good basis for later meditation exercises. One must be able to build on something that can later mature in a more differentiated form.

Even today there are numerous esotericists who attribute magical powers to this place in the Dragon Wall. Even if they do not make the devil responsible for it any more, but very special natural forces and events, which have mythical-meditative character with it. I cannot agree with this. As I have already explained, there is no look which lifts me above the tableau of the Other so far that I can speak with Him. But only this can be the meaning of it all, to have a part of the 'trialogue', an illuminating and revealing conversation, a real 'saying' with this wonderful painting of nature or in myself (pass-, identity-word). The 'magical places of power' do not begin to discuss themselves. They exist, as well as there are the angels, but they all have no message for us. This comes only with the pass-word and its interpretation.

The view of the two mountains and the lake from the northern heights is undoubtedly more meditative, even though I like to remember the exciting stories of the devil's flight. As a child one lives much more in the 'perception identity' and not in the 'thinking identity' as I distinguished it at the beginning following Freud. The mask, which the mother holds in front of her face, puts it into panic. When a beloved object is suddenly hidden, the child bursts into tears. How good that as adults we no longer have to do this, but an occasional mourning, an 'inner weeping' as some call it, would not hurt us. Allowing 'inner' and thus invisible tears concentrates the body image and pulls it back together at the intersection of the axes. The oriental wailers master this body methodology well, they are not hysterical, lamenting women. They simply genuinely give vent to a relief, which is not only justified because of a person to be mourned, but also because of the sad fate of their own, and also of the whole world. Tears also belong to the 'enjoying substance', to the 'jouissance'.

You can't meditate without including the world around you, and it's usually in a bad state. A short melancholic state is often helpful, one reacts off. So also something like that must not be missing sometimes in meditation. With the 'jouissance feminine' I have described this reference of a feeling which is definitely enjoyment and yet also includes pain. Perhaps it could be described as a kind of wistfulness or devotion that is for the Other in one's inner being, for the stranger, but also for the 'Id-You' in oneself, for one's counter-occupied otherness in the unconscious, in the transcendent. For the development of the full personality - writes sociologist T. Lipowatz - individuation and love of transcendence are needed, both are necessary.[66]

Lipowatz warns against "letting the action of man be absorbed in so-called processes of history, that is, in historians' or social analyses. He describes the existence of a 'fear of individuation', the fear of a deep, inner lack, which on the one hand can only be eliminated by a complex individuation process by means of self-conquest or meditation. On the other hand, a love of transcendence is also necessary. I have already pointed out this devotion to the unconscious, to the other in oneself, in the discussion about love as a category of cognition and in the

---

[66] Lipowatz, T., Die Verleugnung des Politischen (The Denial oft he Political), Quadriga (1986).

science subordinated to 'love'. This Other can be the early man as well as the child, as well as the fascination of the other sex, the 'Id-Thou' or as well as the 'trialogue' taking place in meditation.

It can also be something body-related, something related to the neuro-psyche, there is only the question how to imagine it, without the real body, without the brain, and yet 'realized' as the Lacanian or Rossetian 'real'. As the real charisma that comes about without one's own making, without one's own manipulating, rising up or sinking down, unfolding in tears, in joy. One has to wait until the perception of an area of one's own body image arises in meditation or the life in dying comes to the fore. In this process, the anatomical body becomes numb, deaf, so that the attention can turn around, turn inward, as in sleep. Gaze and hearing turn around in such a way that they 'see' into the concave mirror of the cerebrum or 'hear' the verbal echoes in vaults of the word centers in the temporal lobe, and so 'eavesdrop' or inwardly 'see' something from the buzzing, murmuring there.

One last example on the nature of pass- and formula-words (see picture above). "Es war Verrrr-Rat" (it was betrrrr-ayel) thought one of my patients after she had practiced only briefly with the described practice formula of RADICIT and two other such formulations' of which the one was VE-RO-RA-TE. The emphasis of the 'r' had clearly struck her, but also the fact that this pass-word had probably been triggered by the almost identical sounding formula-word (VE-RO-RA-TE) seemed very plausible to her. Thus from both sides the power of the symbolic order in the unconscious is shown. The letters of VE-R and RA-T, which are strongly determined by the 'crystalline', but also contain clearly word-like, symbolic, may still have had a metonymic effect, when they became "Verrrr-Rat" (betrrrr-ayel) in the next moment of a meditation that went a little further into the depths, thus reaching a now 'linguistically' stronger, metaphorical expression.

But not only this purely formal clarity and concreteness was interesting, also the meaning of 'betrayal' had an important background. Her husband had betrayed her, that is, cheated on her, which she had already suspected, but at that moment it became a certainty to her. Thus strengthened, she could definitely confront her husband, and he, dumbfounded, admitted what she had suspected. It is not uncommon for someone to suspect something and yet not want to know the truth for years. But strengthened by such a stirring word, the situation changes. Now this is not always as blatant as in another example where a man suddenly heard or thought "Murderer!" while practicing. He was genuinely startled and confused by this. But the matter was quickly resolved.

First of all, as in any good psychoanalysis, he had a negative transference; he didn't want to take away from me that my procedure works and show me what dangerous situations it can put one in. He would have taken the pass-word as a call for a suicide, he said. But wasn't there a 'murderer' in him, namely definitely one of himself, as is also implied in Heimito von Doderer's novel 'Ein Mord, den jeder begeht' ('A murder that everyone commits'). Self-hatred and self-doubt tormented him very much, and the association with the 'murderer' was not so bad. In the end, they brought him to the conclusion that he could also change his life as a perpetrator and victim by making a new start, not murderously, but 'trialogically'.

For the 'trialogue' always includes death. Death or nothingness is the most animated signifier in every speech, in every dialogue and in every psychoanalysis, where the therapist has to symbolize it or in meditation, where one suffers it imaginarily. But also the real death people usually die so unspecial, so meaningless. I do not mean that thousands should accompany one on the last way and say goodbye with pomp and glory. I'm thinking more of an Indian saying that goes, 'At your birth you cried out, at your death let others cry.' So in the meantime you should have moved something, it should have been a 180 degree change or at least a part of it. So the third partner in the 'trialogue' could also always be this, this Other, of which one never quite knows whether he/she is alive or dead. The effect lies in the otherness, it is a life while dying, either way.

After all these chapters I cannot contribute more to the essence of 'trialogy'. Everyone has to take the last step himself, even if we are increasingly used to the fact that there are always specialists somewhere who know everything. The world is spinning so fast. In her book 'they know everything' the author Y. Hofstetter shows how the reliance on digitalization and computer technology has led to catastrophes (e.g. the shooting down of an Iran-Air passenger plane in 1988). And in J. Ronson's book 'So You've Been Publicly Shamed' is the story of a woman who, by making an ironic remark on Twitter, triggered a shitstorm that ruined her life. Two examples of modern nightmares that will become commonplace in the future. What used to be oppression and existential hardship is now becoming insanity. So horrors will always exist, which is why meditation is so necessary.

20. Appendix

The meditative procedure I have developed and often quoted in the text I have called Analytic Psychocatharsis and published in numerous books, lectures and internet articles. It is the twentieth ascent of the mountain. One can use the procedure on one's own, the attendance of an introductory course is not absolutely necessary. Once one understands it intellectually and has read the description of the practice as described in the last section, but in more detail at www.analytic-psychocatharsis.com, one can also have practical experience with it. As mentioned one sits best in comfortable attitude and repeats purely mentally (possibly with closed or half-closed eyes) three or four of the formula-words monotonously one after the other (at the end of the last one one starts again with the first one).

This causes an increasingly deeper relaxation and a cathartic experience develops, e.g. a 'trickling through' in the body image or a perception of its brightness, in short: an 'Id Rays'. After about twenty minutes - especially when a cathartic, liberating experience has developed - one begins with the second exercise by concentrating inwardly upwardly or rightwardly in the head, listening inwardly and listening until a 'sound', something 'sounding', an 'Id Speaks' occurs, which basically contains one's own, unconscious thoughts, which seem to come from the depths or from a distance. This right-sided hearing of thoughts has something to do with the more prosodic speech center, which also participates in the image-real.

The events named pass-words then represent the more analytical part of the process, because they can be easily interpreted as word-real, as answers from the unconscious.

An intellectual understanding of the method is also important, because the scientific structure requires it, but this also gives support and security during practical practice. Other methods fall back on mythical-mystical foundations and so one must either cling to the personality of the teacher or bow to the theoretical background, which comes from religious-confessional or purely imagined ideas. Certainly, the pass-words, which ultimately contribute most to the 'trialogue', do not represent an entirely easy-to-handle method. They need to be reworked by ratio. As I was finishing this book, another such password came to me, "They always just say 'seven.'" To me, that was immediately an obvious phrase, which to an outsider is probably hokum. However, I asked a few people what they associated with it and thought of it.

Mostly a comparable result came out as it was coherent for me. The 'seven' is valid in mythical contexts, like some other of the first whole numbers also, as a special number. Since there is still no empirical theory of the first numbers, it is easy to understand that the three, the four, the seven and the ten, for example, have taken certain special roles. Even Euclid said for this reason, which is equally valid today in set theory, that one must start counting with the 'many'. So even in the most exact science, that of mathematics, we have no absolutely firm ground under our feet.

But in the end it has to do with the number only to the half. Rather I am myself meant with it with those who always only say: It behaves in such a way or in such a way, always only the same is said: always only they say 'seven'. The 'seven' as the lowest generator number, the seven dwarfs, the seven wonders of the world, the seven days of the creation myth and Wittgenstein's seventh day, the Sunday, as the day of the 'trialog', have probably only played a little part here for the production of my pass-word. Quite a few other references occurred to me as well. I always say the same thing in my books, that's the mistake. For me, this event was important. That's the point of the process. No one else could have told me that. Yes, probably no one at all would have thought of telling me something like that in this form.

Bibliography

Baggini, J., Ich denke, also will ich, (I think, so I want) dtv (2016)

Barkhaus, A., Mayer, M., Identität, Leiblichkeit, Normativität (identity, corporeality, normativity(Suhrkamp (1996)

Bauriedl, T., Beziehungsanalyse, (relationship analysis) Suhrkamp (1993)

Benthien, C., Wulf, Ch., Körperteile (body parts), Rowohlt (2001)

Bezzel, C., Wittgenstein, Junius (1996)

Breuer, R., Immer Ärger mit dem Urknall (Always Trouble with the Big Bang), Rowohlt (1993)

Brockman, J., Vogel, S., Wie funktioniert die Welt? (How does the world work), Fischer Taschenbuch (2013)

Byung-Chul Han, Die Austreibung des Anderen (The Expulsion of the Other), Fischer Wissenschaft (201)

Byung-Chul Han, Die Errettung des Schönen (The Salvation of Beauty), Fischer Wissenschaft (201)

Camus, A., Der Mythos des Sisyphos, Rowohlt (2018)

Carnap, R., Einführung in die Philosophie der Naturwissenschaft (Introduction to the Philosophy of Natural Science) (1969)

Damasio, A. R., Descartes` Irrtum, Dtv (1997)

Dennet, D. C., Von den Bakterien zu Bach – und zurück, Suhrkamp (2018)

Davies, P., Gott und die moderne Physik (God and modern physics), Bert. M. (1986)

Eccles, J. C., Gehirn und Seele, Piper (1987)

Eichmeier, J., Höfer, O., Endogene Bildmuster, U&S — Verlag (1974)

Fischer-Lichte, E., Performativität: Eine Einführung, transcript (2012)

Freud, S., Studienausgabe, Fischer (1989)

Görz, G., Einführung in die Künstliche Intelligenz (Introduction to Artificial Intelligence), Addison-Wesley (1996)

Harari, Y. N., Homo Deus, C. H. Beck (2017)

Heidegger, M., Unterwegs zur Sprache, G. Neske (1959)

Hofstadter, D., Die Analogie, Klett-Cotta (2014)

Hustvedt, S., Die gleissende Welt (The blazing Wiorld) Rowohlt (2016)

Husttvedt, S., Das Leiden eines Amerikanmers, Rowohlt (2009)

Hustvedt, S., Wenn Gefühle auf Worte treffen (When feelings meet words) , Kampa (2019)

Jacobs, A., Schrott, R., Gehirn und Gedicht, Hanser (2011

Jakobson, R., Semiotik, Suhrkamp (1988)

Jakobson, R., On Language, Harvard University Press (1995)

Jung. C.G., Gesammelte Werke, Walter (1983)

Kant, I., Kritik der reinen Vernunft, Reclam (1966)

Kluge, F., Etymologisches Wörterbuch, W. de Gruyter (1989)

Lacan, J., Schriften I - III, Walter, (1975)

Lacan, J., Seminare I,I, VII, XI, XX, Quadriga (1980-1995)

Lacan, J., Seminaire Nr. III, Iv, VIII, XVII, Edition Seuil (1981-1994)

Lacan, J., Die Bildungen des Unbewussten, Turia & Kant (2006)

Lacan, J., Mitschriften der Seminare,VI,IX,X,XII,XV, B.R.L.F., Strasbourg

Laplanche, J., Pontalis, J. B., Das Vokabular Der Psychoanalyse, Suhrkamp (1989)

Merleau-Ponty, M., Das Sichtbare und das Unsichtbare (The Visible and the Invisible) Fink Verlag (1994)

Plato, Sämtliche Werke, Insel Verlag (1991)

Popper, K. R., Eccles, J. C., Das Ich und sein Gehirn (The Ego and it's Brain), Piper (1989)

Potthoff, P., Die Begegnung der Subjekte (The Encounter of Subjects), Psychosozial-Verlag (2014)

Roazen, D., Der innere Sinn, Archäologie eines Gefühls (The Inner Touch, Archaeology of Feeling), Fischer (2012)

Roheim, G., Die Panik der Götter (The Panic of the Gods), Kindler (1975)

Rosset, C., Das Reale in seiner Einzigartigkeit (The real in its uniqueness), Merve (2000)

Schmidt-Hellerau, C., Lebenstrieb & Todestrieb (Life Drive & Death Drive), Libido & Lethe, Verlag Intern. Psychoanalyse (1995)

Searle, J. R., Geist, Hirn und Wissenschaft, Suhrkamp (1992)

Seidler, G. H., Der Blick des Anderen (The View of the Other), Verlag Intern, Psychoanalyse (1995)

Strowik, E., Sprechende Körper (Speaking Bodies), Fink-Verlag (2009)

Thorne, K. S., Gekrümmter Raum und Verbogene Zeit, Knaur (1996)

Tipler, F. J., Über die Omegapunkttheorie, Piper (1994)

Uexküll, Th., Fuchs, M., Subjektive Anatomie, Schattauer (1994)

Weiss, Der Andere in der Übertragung (The Other in Transference), Frommann-Holzboog, (1988)

Weizsäcker, C. F. von, Die Einheit der Natur (The Unity of Nature), Dtv (1995)

Wilhelm, R., Informatik, C.H.Beck (1996)

Wolf, F. A., Die Physik der Träume (Physic of the Dreams), Byblos (1996)

Wygotski, L.S., Denken und 'Sprechen (Thinking and 'Speaking)', Fischer (1981)

Books published in English by the author

The physically sick Soul

In this booklet of only forty pages, the author describes in a simplified form the method of *Analytic Psychocatharsis* that he developed. It is not only about the mentally ill soul, but also about the treatment of the disorder expressed in a more physical form.

What about the ONE

The One is only insufficiently described in mathematics. It is about the spiritual-physical unity of man, which can only be achieved through a combination of psychoanalytical and meditative exercises. The author describes this process using the literature of Siri Hustvedt and other female authors as well as the psychoanalysis of J. Lacan.

A Path to self-analytical Practice

The vertical Ego

Our usual social Ego is oriented horizontally, but the essential and still predominantly unconscious Ego is oriented in the vertical. This is connected with primary inner psychic reflections, which are not exactly captured by psychoanalysis, because it is more oriented to the word. With a few meditative exercises one can reach the sufficiently good vertical and unite it with the horizontal.

Life while Dying, a treatise on Sisyphus and on a new Self-practice for today

Outsmarting Death two Times.

Sisyphus managed to outsmart death twice before he finally had to roll the big stone up the hill in Hades. Today's man has it better, for whom in the meantime it is proven that after his medically determined death still brain activities are perceptible. By the procedure of the analytic psychocatharsis he can use them to postpone the death by an important experience.

List of other works of the author from MCS-Verlag in German

Herz-Sprache, Eine Psychoanalyse des Herzens

Politik / Therapie, Begreifen, was man schon weiß - wie Politik therapeutisch zu denken wäre

Das autochthone Genießen, Essays zu einem neuen selbstanalytischen Verfahren

Siddharthas Wiederkehr, Ein wissenschaftlicher Roman – eine Anregung zur Selbstanalyse

Nach Lacan, Über Physik, Psychoanalyse und die Metapher des Genießens – eine Selbstpraxis

interhot, Gespräche mit dem Unbewussten

Das Gerade und das Gekrümmte, Die Behandlung einer Psychose

Die Mathematik des Eros, Die ‚perfektoiden Räume‘ des Unbewussten – eine Selbstpraxis

Psychoanalyse / Meditation, Eine Broschüre zu Theorie und Praxis der *Analytischen Psychokatharsis*

Platons Lieb-ido, Ein wissenschaftlicher Roman – eine Überredung zur Selbsttherapie

Überwältigt, Psychische Strategie und Meditation